ROUTLEDGE LIBRARY EDITIONS:
FINANCIAL MARKETS

Volume 12

CAPITAL MOBILIZATION AND REGIONAL FINANCIAL MARKETS

CAPITAL MOBILIZATION AND REGIONAL FINANCIAL MARKETS

The Pacific Coast States, 1850 – 1920

KERRY A. ODELL

Routledge
Taylor & Francis Group
LONDON AND NEW YORK

First published in 1992 by Garland Publishing, Inc.

This edition first published in 2018
by Routledge
2 Park Square, Milton Park, Abingdon, Oxon OX14 4RN

and by Routledge
711 Third Avenue, New York, NY 10017

Routledge is an imprint of the Taylor & Francis Group, an informa business

British Library Cataloguing in Publication Data
A catalogue record for this book is available from the British Library

ISBN: 978-1-138-56537-1 (Set)
ISBN: 978-0-203-70248-2 (Set) (ebk)
ISBN: 978-1-138-56645-3 (Volume 12) (hbk)
ISBN: 978-1-315-12372-1 (Volume 12) (ebk)

Publisher's Note
The publisher has gone to great lengths to ensure the quality of this reprint but points out that some imperfections in the original copies may be apparent.

Disclaimer
The publisher has made every effort to trace copyright holders and would welcome correspondence from those they have been unable to trace.

Capital Mobilization and Regional Financial Markets

The Pacific Coast States, 1850 – 1920

KERRY A. ODELL

GARLAND PUBLISHING, INC.
NEW YORK & LONDON
1992

Library of Congress Cataloging-in-Publication Data

Odell, Kerry A.
Capital mobilization and regional financial markets : the Pacific Coast states, 1850-1920 / Kerry A. Odell.
p. cm. — (The Financial sector of the American economy)
Originally presented as the author's thesis (doctoral)—University of California, Berkeley, 1987.
Includes bibliographical references and index.
ISBN 0-8153-0959-7
1. Capital market—Pacific States—History. 2. Finance—San Francisco Region—History. I. Title. II. Series.
HG5127.033 1992
332.63'2'09795—dc20 92-27793
CIP

Printed on acid-free, 250-year-life paper
Manufactured in the United States of America

To my mother and father,
with gratitude for their wisdom,
support, and unconditional love.

CONTENTS

TABLES

PREFACE

This work originally appeared as my doctoral dissertation in Economics at the University of California, Berkeley, in 1987. It was a reaction to the observation that much of the research on national capital market integration in nineteenth-century America has focused on the reduction in average interest differentials between New York City and large, arbitrarily defined regions in the United States. Such analyses tend to ignore the level of financial development within regions. Instead, they rely upon explanations of differential barriers to capital flows *between* regions.

In contrast, this study argues that barriers to financial flows *within* regions may be as important in affecting capital flows as interregional barriers. Regional markets allow efficient mobilization of local funds, which is crucial if a region is isolated from outside funds sources and must depend on existing local savings supplies. Furthermore, established financial markets within a region can act both as sources of information for prospective lenders outside the region and as transactions channels for funds inflows. Consequently, regional markets can lower the cost of providing funds to an unfamiliar region, and thus promote national financial market integration.

The analytical framework developed here motivates an investigation of regional financial development in the Pacific Coast states between 1850 and 1920. A regional commercial network centered on San Francisco extended into California, Oregon, and Washington; this formed the basis for a financial market which recycled wealth (largely from San Francisco and California residents) into enterprises throughout the region. The market also facilitated the inflow of funds from the eastern United States, particularly from Chicago. For the period between 1880 and 1911, econometric tests of interest rate sensitivity and convergence are performed, using both short-term and long-term interest rates. The results indicate much closer financial relationships between San Francisco and the Coast states than between the Pacific Coast region and urban centers in the Northeast.

The study concludes with conjectures about the American South. It appears that the South's stagnation between the Civil War and World War I may have resulted from the region's failure to develop an internal financial market. New Orlean's external orientation and the dispersion of savers and investors inhibited the formation of a centralized market within the region. This, in turn, made the recycling of local funds difficult, and the importation of funds costly.

While a great deal of research remains to be done on the issues of financial development, I hope this work will reiterate the importance of spatial factors in that development. Furthermore, the consideration of regional urban hierarchies in capital mobilization will help tie together microeconomic and macroeconomic analyses of the development question.

ACKNOWLEDGMENTS

This research is the product of many contributors. Richard Sutch first helped to formulate the specific question and to place it in a broader context. Albert Fishlow provided valuable assistance on style and methodology; Harry Scheiber improved the study's historical analysis. Earlier drafts benefitted from input by James Pierce, Joan Hannon, Roger Ransom, Lance Davis, and Richard Sylla. Janet Ceglowski offered both moral support and detailed, insightful comments during the course of the original work.

I would like to thank John James of the University of Virginia, whose interest rate data is central to the econometric analysis of market formation presented here. Philip Forstall of Rand McNally Company kindly provided archival data unavailable elsewhere. Financial support was received from the University of California and the U.C. Intercampus Group in Economic History; much of the dissertation was conceived during a year's fellowship at the Bancroft Library. A faculty sabbatical fellowship from Scripps College and a Stevenson Foundation grant freed my time to rework parts of the manuscript.

The Scripps College community has been of great help. Nancy Burson's endless cheerfulness and the patience of Nancy Krimmer and Karmel Clark transformed the manuscript from an ugly duckling to something more resembling a swan. My friend and colleague Patricia Dillon has been an invaluable cheerleader throughout.

Finally, I wish to acknowledge the large debt I owe my family. Their loyalty and sense of humor kept the work in perspective.

Capital Mobilization and Regional Financial Markets

CHAPTER 1

Introduction

One of the more serious challenges faced in the world economy today is the development of Third World and newly-industrializing countries. In these nations, rapid population growth provides a large labor force, but the youth of the population creates a relatively low level of savings. At the same time, large amounts of residentiary, infrastructural, and industrial capital are needed. As a consequence of small savings accumulations and a high marginal product of capital, there is concern about methods for exporting capital to the developing countries. However, international lending is not very effective to countries that have no means with which to distribute funds to projects outside major urban areas.

Similar concerns arose in the United States during the nineteenth and early twentieth centuries. Throughout this period, population and economic activity shifted to the west and south, away from developed eastern centers where much of the accumulated savings were located. The problem encountered in these newer regions was two-fold: how to most efficiently recycle indigenous savings, and how to attract and distribute funds from the east. The bulk of the literature in economic history has only partly addressed the latter question--how were funds attracted from the east? The answer is usually couched in terms of the date of "national capital market integration," and considers vaguely defined costs of funds transfer between broad regions of the United States. Chapter 2 discusses this literature on the capital market question.

The inadequacy of previous work lies in its failure to address the issue of financial markets *within* the developing regions. This issue has two important implications for patterns of regional growth and development. First, such markets allow the most efficient use of available local savings, thus maximizing per capita incomes when no capital imports are possible. But these internal markets also facilitate imports of capital and lower the costs of distributing such capital throughout a region; previous research has not recognized this. Regional markets act as intermediaries or agents for outside savers; thus, national capital market integration should be more correctly envisioned as the linkage of regional markets.

The importance of such markets can be highlighted by considering the consequences of the absence of these markets. For a new region isolated from outside savings, the absence of an internal financial market means that it will be difficult to transfer available savings to the most productive use in the region,[1] and regional growth will be limited. In addition, if outside funds are able to flow in to some point (usually the major city or port of the region), the mobilization of those funds from that location to the rest of the region will be difficult and costly for the outside saver, reducing his incentive to export funds to the region.

Clearly, the level of internal market formation will be key in patterns of regional growth and development. Whether such markets form or not will depend on a number of factors relating to urban patterns, commercial networks (which provide transaction and information channels) and the distribution of savings and investment opportunities in the region. Based upon notions of economic geography, location theory, and empirical evidence from American history, Chapter 3 defines a conceptual framework for the role of regional markets in capital mobilization and for the economic foundations which determine the extent of financial market development within a region.

This framework is applied to the economic history of the Pacific Coast region of the United States. This region developed in the late nineteenth and early twentieth centuries, in a location far-removed from the financial center of New York City. Chapter 4 illustrates the dominant role of San Francisco and San Francisco merchants in commercial patterns on the Coast. The networks of information and the mercantile wealth centered on San Francisco represented the foundations of the financial market which spanned the Pacific Coast region by the early 1880s. Chapter 5 discusses some of the institutions--commercial banks, bank correspondents, life insurance companies, and stock exchanges--which were headquartered in San Francisco and which had links throughout the region. These institutional networks were the successors of informal, personal financial ties, and they mobilized regional savings into agricultural, industrial, and infrastructural projects throughout the region.

Because of the difficulty involved in gauging actual capital flows through these institutions, Chapter 6 uses measures of interest rate coordination within the region to estimate the level of market integration. The primary data base used is a series on national bank loan interest rates estimated by John James for the period 1888 to 1911. Using this series, measures of market integration, including interest rate correlation and convergence, are calculated for San Francisco and her regional hinterland. The results indicate a high level of financial integration between San Francisco and California, Oregon, and Washington. This regional market performed in isolation from New York City until the early years of the twentieth century; the primary source of outside finance appears to have been Chicago.

San Francisco's ability to mobilize funds (whether home savings or capital imports) to points throughout the Pacific Coast region gave her an essential role in maintaining high levels of per capita income in the region during the nineteenth and twentieth centuries. The regional market controlled by San Francisco was the starting point for this city's status as one of the three primary financial centers in the United States today.

This work concludes with some conjectures about the puzzle of postbellum Southern stagnation. Using the conceptual framework developed here, it is suggested that one cause of this stagnation was the failure to form a regional financial market. The lack of a clear regional metropolis, scattered savings supplies, and weak regional trade networks mitigated against the development of such a market. The results were an inability to efficiently mobilize local savings, and difficulty in attracting and distributing imports of mobile capital. Stagnation and isolation from a national capital market were the consequences for the southern region of the United States through the 1930s.

NOTES

1. This assumes savers are not the best investors of funds.

CHAPTER 2

The Missing Geography of Capital Markets

For total output of an economy to grow, there must be increases in the amounts of inputs, or there must be improvements in technology. For output per capita to increase--for there to be "economic growth"--the amount of capital goods available per worker must increase.[1] Thus, the accumulation of capital, by channelling resources out of consumption and into investment, is a key feature in the process of economic growth. This is especially true from a policy-making point of view, since the accumulation of capital is a factor more easily controlled by governmental bodies than are changes in technology or labor force participation rates.

CAPITAL MOBILIZATION AND ECONOMIC GROWTH

While the accumulation of capital is important in economic growth, the mobilization of that capital is equally important. Sooner or later, it becomes apparent that those people who are "good savers"--who have earned income in excess of their consumption expenditures--are not necessarily the best judges of how to employ those savings in investment projects. This separation quickly becomes apparent in an economy which is expanding spatially and sectorally.

Here, a surplus unit (saver) may be far removed in place or experience from the projects in which capital would have the highest return. In this case, while the size of the total savings stream is an important determinant of growth, the direction of the stream will determine how large an increase in output will be obtained from the savings.

It is for these reasons that attention is turned from the accumulation of physical capital to the mobilization of savings which can purchase capital. Here, the issue of financial markets arises. Under the assumption of differing entrepreneurial talent in the employment of savings or under the assumption of economies of scale in investment, it is possible to conceive of a world in which output per capita can be increased merely by the specialization of savers and investors.[2] Financial development allows such specialization by creating markets which facilitate the trade of current purchasing power for the promise of higher purchasing power in the future.

"Market" may be a strong term for the many types of relationships which arise to transfer capital funds from one person to another. In fact, it is probably more reasonable to consider an entire spectrum of financial "arrangements".[3] Davis and North's 1971 work represents a return to the notion that the parameters of an economy, within which production takes place, are not static. Rather, the institutional structure is both a dynamic and an influential force which determines the size and allocation of the economic pie. Douglas Dowd went so far as to say that "the core of the developmental problem is institutional. This is not to overlook the obvious fact that resources, natural and human, must be obtainable if things are to be produced. But the mere presence of a 'good' resource base does not ensure economic development."[4]

A wide range of authors has discussed the importance of institutions which promote the finance of capital formation through facilitating the transfer of savings into investment. John Gurley and Edward Shaw elaborate on the spectrum of financial development, from self-finance in a Robinson Crusoe economy through the direct finance of brokered loans, and finally to the world of complex financial intermediaries who issue indirect debt of their own.[5] Raymond Goldsmith believes that, while financial development and economic development are correlated, one can assume no causal link.[6] Another group of economists has focused on the role of banks in economic growth and development. Joseph Schumpeter acknowledges that, without bankers who could grant credit to entrepreneurs, economic development might never occur. Without command over existing resources, an entrepreneur would not be able to undertake "new combinations."[7] Alexander Gerschenkron and Rondo Cameron also explore the role of banks as initiators of, or as responders to, industrialization in historical periods.[8] Work by Nathaniel Leff and Naomi Lamoreaux, on the other hand, investigates the informal "kinship" groups which substitute for financial markets in newly developing countries.[9] Finally, returning to the Gurley and Shaw tradition, Ronald McKinnon focuses upon current developing countries and assigns a large role to the capital market within such countries.

> To say that there are "imperfections in factor markets" is distressingly vague and often signals the end of formal economic analysis. But further systematic inquiry can proceed if the neoclassical approach of treating labor, land, and capital symmetrically as primary factors is dropped. It is hypothesized here that fragmentation in the capital market--endemic in the under-developed environment without carefully considered public policy--causes the misuse of labor and land, suppresses entrepreneurial development, and condemns important sectors of the economy to inferior technologies.[10]

AMERICAN CAPITAL FORMATION AND MOBILIZATION

The economic history of the United States between 1850 and 1920 has provided useful material for the study of the development of financial institutions. Tremendous expansion occurred which challenged existing financial relationships to mobilize savings into capital formation. Through immigration and natural population growth, the labor force increased by almost six hundred percent. The amount of available land was multiplied seven times, as the territorial expansion of the United States was completed and as the transfer of land from the government to private citizens continued. To complement these large increases in human and natural resources, there was a 47-fold increase in the American capital stock between 1850 and 1920. The increases in the total amount of resources available, along with the increased productivity of factors of production, resulted in net national product rising more than 1800 percent in this period.[11]

During the period 1870 to 1910, it has been estimated that the capital stock accounted for 23 percent of the increase in net national product in the United States (capital's share between 1840 and 1860 is estimated to be 26 percent), trailing labor's relative share of 46 percent, and equalling the contribution of residual productivity.[12] This residual includes technological change embodied in the capital stock, and institutional improvements such as financial markets which made capital accumulation and mobilization more efficient. On a per capita basis, the importance of the capital stock is even greater. Edward Denison estimates that 35 percent of per capita growth in the United States between 1909 and 1929 was the result of increases in the capital stock.[13] This percentage is likely to be even higher for the period 1850 to 1920, when capital was more scarce relative to labor and natural resources.

The accumulation and mobilization of capital takes on even more telling characteristics when some of these figures are disaggregated by region or industry. During this period, there was a broad movement of activity out of agriculture and the eastern United States, and into manufacturing and the western United States. Between 1870 and 1910, the percentage of the labor force engaged in resource-oriented activities (agriculture, mining, fishing, forestry, and logging) fell from 53 to 35 percent, while the proportion of labor involved in manufacturing rose from 12 to 28 percent. The service sector increased its share of the labor force from 25 to 38 percent.[14] The percentage of total value-added by agriculture declined from 59 to 33 percent between 1849 and 1899, while manufacturing's share of total value-added increased from 32 to 49 percent.[15]

At the same time that the manufacturing and service sectors were advancing, population and economic activity were shifting westward. The eastern United States (the Northeast and North Central regions) contained 36 percent of total population in 1860, but only 30 percent in 1920. The west's share of population (in the area from the Rocky Mountains to the Pacific) rose from 2 to 9 percent. During the same period, the share of total personal income received by the Northeast and North Central regions of the country fell from 50 to 39 percent, while the west's share rose from 4 to 10 percent.[16]

FINANCIAL DEVELOPMENT IN THE UNITED STATES

These spatial and sectoral shifts made the development of financial institutions essential. While it would be difficult to summarize the state of personal financial relationships during this period (other than to note the success of financiers such as J.P. Morgan), we do have evidence on the increasing importance of more formal financial markets. First, the period begins and ends with the two most significant excursions by the federal government into the financial system. In 1863, the first National Bank Act was passed by Congress, ostensibly to correct the ills of a segmented banking system and a non-uniform national currency. Fifty years later, the Federal Reserve System was established, in part to resolve some of the problems of the earlier system. Throughout the period, there was also an expansion of state regulation of banking, with respect to incorporation, note issue, branching, and so on.

Some rough statistics may give an idea of the expansion of formal financial institutions between 1850 and 1920. In 1850, there were 824 banks in the United States, with assets of just over 500 million dollars. By 1920, these figures had grown to 31,000 banks with assets of 54 billion dollars.[17] Meanwhile, insurance companies (which were destined to become some of the most powerful financial institutions in the country) experienced rapid growth. There were only 43 life insurance companies in the United States in 1854, with total sales of 15 million dollars. In 1920, there were 335 companies with annual sales of more than nine billion dollars.[18] While these statistics indicate that the spectrum of financial institutions in the United States broadened in the late nineteenth and early twentieth centuries, they are mute on the question of whether these institutions mobilized capital to expanding sectors and regions. The opportunities open in the developing regions of the South and the West are obvious in the rates of return available on investments in those areas. Research has estimated that the return on manufacturing capital in 1860 was 28 percent in the West, and 26 percent in the South, while it was roughly 22 percent in the East.[19] Fogel and Rutner estimate that, in 1899, returns on agricultural capital were 21.9 percent in the Pacific, and 12.4 percent in the South--the highest returns in the country.[20] Clearly, there were profits to be made by mobilizing funds to these developing regions.

The neoclassical tradition in economics leads us to expect a wide range of well-functioning markets that mobilize all types of goods and resources. Each market is arbitraged across time and space, leaving no long-lasting unexploited profit opportunities. Financial markets, however, merit special consideration since finance involves trading current purchasing power not for a tangible commodity, but for the promise of purchasing power to be returned some time in the future. Because of this temporal element, uncertainty and risk are important factors in financial market performance.

When reliable information on investment opportunities is not forthcoming, or when there are no established channels through which opportunities can be searched for and negotiated, the size of a financial market will be limited. As August Lösch, the prominent location theorist, has pointed out, the distance between borrower and lender is "in the final analysis," responsible for the factors of uncertainty, risk, and transactions costs which raise the price of finance.[21] The lender wants to charge an interest rate which, net of risk and liquidity premiums and transactions costs, equals or exceeds his rate of time preference. Thus, the larger such premiums and costs are for loans to distant borrowers, the higher will be the interest rate offered to the borrower. At some distance from the lender, there will be no borrowers willing to accept loans at the offered rate. This is, in effect, the geographical limit of the financial market, because no funds will be requested, at the offered rate, by borrowers more distant from the lender.

Work in economic history before and after World War I placed a great deal of emphasis on the geographical aspects of market structure and economic behavior. For example, Gras' *An Introduction to Economic History* [1922] primarily discusses the stages of metropolitan development, with particular emphasis on the relationships between cities and hinterlands and a focus on sub-national markets. The concern with spatial factors in economics has been carried on by economic geographers such as Allan Pred, James Vance, William Code, and Michael Conzen, but the neoclassical tradition has, until recently, discouraged much work on geographical delimitations within current economic research.

The debate about the timing of the development of a national capital market in the United States has been one of the more long-lived discussions in the economic history literature; the first articles on the question appeared in the 1890s. The contributions to this debate have followed the general outlines of contemporary economics of the time, with a greater emphasis on spatial finance in earlier works, and less importance attached to geographical considerations in current work. Despite rather different approaches and emphases on spatial relationships, most of the participants have investigated the development of a national market by looking at interest rate differentials between regions of the United States,[22] and by measuring the decline of these differentials over time.

One of the first authors to examine the ability of American capital markets and financial institutions to transfer funds is D.M. Frederiksen. Frederiksen uses 1890 United States Census data on mortgage rates to illustrate the large interest differentials between eastern mortgages, and mortgages in the South and the Midwest. He also collects information on the ownership of mortgage debt in Alabama, Tennessee, Kansas, Illinois, and Iowa. His study finds that 59 percent of mortgages were held by residents of the states, and that only twenty percent were held by resident or non-resident financial institutions.[23] Frederiksen's work suggests that financial institutions were not very active in mobilizing capital across state lines in the 1890s, and that the result was a very segmented mortgage market within the United States.

Investigating the short-term market at the turn of the century, R.M. Breckenridge uses national bank discount rates on first-class double-name commercial paper, as reported by Bradstreet correspondents. Looking at the period from 1893 to 1897, he notes that southern and western borrowers might pay, on average, an interest rate three to six percentage points higher than paid by eastern borrowers. For example, the average rate paid in San Francisco was more than 6.2 percent, while borrowers in Boston were paying as little as 3.8 percent.[24] Breckenridge dismisses risk differentials as an explanation for these interest rate differentials; he believes that the discount rates were quoted on paper of standard quality. Instead, he attributes the higher rates in the South and the West to a "disinclination of capital to migrate," and he speculates that the prohibition of nationwide branch banking was the probable cause.[25]

The advance of the "new economic history" which combined neoclassical theory with improved historical data collection created a whole new group of participants in the national capital market development debate. Breckenridge's conclusion was challenged seventy years later in a paper by Lance Davis.[26] Davis calculates regional averages of gross and net rates of return on the earning assets of national banks between 1870 and 1914. Totals for earning assets (bonds, stock, securities, loans and discounts) are obtained from balance sheets, and gross and net earnings from income statements collected by the Comptroller of the Currency. Davis contends that these earning rates are fairly good proxies for the average interest rates earned by the national banks. While he agrees with Breckenridge that interest rates differed between the large Comptroller-defined regions of the United States (as listed in Figure 2.1 of the Appendix). Davis claims that funds were being mobilized through the developing commercial paper market. Thus, the need for nationwide branch banking was obviated by the spread of commercial paper dealers who could sell western and southern paper to savers in the financial centers of the East. Interest differentials were declining as a result, although rates were not equalized nationwide even as late as 1914.

Many papers followed Davis which criticized his technique for constructing an interest rate series, his choice of the financial actor which was mobilizing funds, or his estimate of the exact timing of integration, but not his basic conclusion of an increasingly integrated national market for funds. Richard Sylla uses the Davis-constructed interest rate series to make a case for the efficiency of funds mobilization within the national banking system. Sylla believes that the bankers' balances which country banks placed with reserve city banks allowed funds to flow from local monopoly banks in agricultural areas to large financial centers. These centers accumulated funds to finance "lumpy" industrial investments. Furthermore, Sylla claims that interest rates declined in the agricultural areas after 1900 when the Gold Standard Act lowered the minimum capital requirements for national banks, thus encouraging the formation of banks in previously monopolized areas.[27]

John James also uses the annual reports of the Comptroller of the Currency, but he calculates a different national bank earning proxy than Davis. By subtracting earnings on stocks, bonds, and bankers' balances, he derives figures which he feels are better measures of the stated (as opposed to realized) interest rate on loans and discounts by national banks. James then constructs a model of interest rate determination based on the capital asset pricing model. He reaches two conclusions. First, he believes that capital market integration resulted from the rise of the commercial paper market (as Davis suggests) and from the rise of the correspondent banking system (as Sylla suggests). He also believes that interest differentials declined in response to a reduction in monopoly power of banks in new regions. Unlike Sylla, however, James sees the formation of state banks in the 1880s as the cause of increased bank competition.[28]

Gene Smiley and Hugh Rockoff take slightly different approaches in analyzing national bank data. Smiley creates a measure of return on "private earning assets" (Davis' earning assets less earnings on United States bonds and bankers' balances), and claims that interest rates were higher in the South and the West because of higher risk premiums attached to assets in those regions. He concludes that declining interest differentials after 1893 resulted from the expansion of the commercial paper market.[29] Rockoff uses national bank profit rates in his analysis, and concludes that high profit rates in the newer regions reflected higher risk of bank failure. Convergence of profit rates occurred as bank failure rates declined in agricultural areas.[30]

One of the latest entries into the national bank earning rate literature comes from Marie Sushka and Brian Barrett. They use the simple Davis regional earning rate to compare the pattern of interest rate movements across the country. Based on tests of information flows between long and short term markets, and between regions, they claim that there was an "unfragmented national market" for funds by the early 1870s. The existence of interregional interest differentials resulted from local bank monopoly power; this monopoly power was broken in the 1870s by the increased availability of alternative business lenders such as the stock market.[31]

Recently, there has been a resurgence of interest in the patterns of mortgage finance. Barry Eichengreen uses mortgage interest rate data from the 1890 Census of the United State to test the relationship of mortgage rates to farm characteristics such as location, size, and crop mix. He concludes that the market was correctly pricing higher risk of southern or western farming in the 1880s, and that interest differentials did not, for the most part, reflect market imperfection. In fact, he believes that the east-west differential may have resulted from eastern rates which were held "too low" by usury ceilings rather than western rates which were "too high."[32] Kenneth Snowden disagrees. He too employs mortgage data from the 1890 Census, but reaches the conclusion that the east-west differentials were not the consequence of higher risk. Instead, he claims that higher rates were paid in the West and the South to cover "the direct costs of moving funds between regions and the uneven diffusion of financial innovation."[33]

The common thread binding all these macroeconomic studies in the new economic history is the use of broad regional aggregates in their interest rate estimates and/or their conclusions about capital mobility. These aggregates, usually based on the Comptroller definitions, do not have any meaning as economic units. They are merely groupings of states which happen to be contiguous. The practice of almost randomly aggregating state level data has been criticized by some authors who research other issues. For example, Robert Sexton questions the regional classification which includes the border states of Kentucky, Tennessee, and Virginia in the "South." He argues that these states are more like the "West," and he shows that some conclusions regarding levels of manufacturing activity and education in the "South" depend on whether or not the border states are included in the regional definition.[34] Even Jeffrey Williamson, one of the most well-known of the cliometricians, warned that "The economic historian, we certainly should have learned by now, aggregates across American regions at very great risk."[35] His cautionary statement would have been more powerful if he had also warned against aggregating *within* regions.

The consolidation of multi-state data is not merely statistical sloppiness; it belies an important assumption about the distribution of returns within the defined regions. By merging separate state-level data points into a regional average, researchers are implicitly assuming that some behavioral relationship exists between interest rates inside the region, so that the level and movement of the average interest rate is a good summary of the financial status of the region in general. In fact, there may be no behavioral relationship between rates in one state and those in another. The average then contains little or no information on financial conditions within the region.[36] If a market *were* in place which mobilized funds throughout a region, we should expect only small interest differentials across the region, and we should expect that movement of interest rates within the region would be coordinated. Under these circumstances, the average of the individual interest rates may be a reasonable generalization of financial conditions in the region. If no market spans the region, however, the distribution of rates of return, and the movements of those rates will be determined by localized supplies and demands for funds. In this case, the "average" rate of return does not represent any meaningful statement about finance throughout the region as a whole. The use of regional aggregates has, therefore, implicitly assumed some market which coordinates financial decisions within the region. John James makes this assumption explicit. He writes, "The period after the Civil War in the United States witnessed a significant narrowing of interest differentials and the gradual merger of local markets into an integrated short-term capital market." He also refers to national market formation as "the trend toward integration of *regional markets*."[37] However, to date, no research has been found which addresses the question of whether or not these regional markets did exist. Vincent Carosso has written a proposal for the study of a regional financial market in the Mid-Atlantic region, but his suggestions were never pursued.[38]

Region-level studies of other markets have been very useful in answering questions of growth and development in American history. Such studies include insightful work on trade flows, such as research by Diane Lindstrom on the Philadelphia region in the early 1800s.[39] Gavin Wright's work on the labor market within the southern United States represents a revolutionary and long-needed study of one kind of regional factor market.[40] It is imperative that economic historians undertake similar region-level studies of financial markets, rather than assume that such markets exist.

Research which models and investigates markets at a regional or sub-regional level has a number of important implications. It can reconcile two conflicting bodies of work: the more microeconomic literature on the power of individual financial institutions[41] and the macroeconomic literature on the integration of a national market. By appealing to the dynamic nature of financial markets, we can see that individual institutions will be powerful in regions without organized financial markets. Over time, however, the entrance of additional institutions improves the mobilization of funds and reduces the impact of individual institutions.

Furthermore, such research would broaden the range of possible explanations for differential patterns of regional growth, and for the differential pace of integration to a national market. Regions which do not develop internal financial markets face two unappealing consequences. First, their ability to mobilize their own savings will be limited. Second, the likelihood that they can attract outside funds and attach to a national market for funds will be bounded by high internal information and transactions costs that extra-regional lenders will also face.

In particular, there are some puzzling observations about the Pacific Coast and the southern regions of the United States which need to be addressed. The Pacific Coast region seemed to quickly attach to the national market for funds after 1900, despite the region's remoteness from the national financial center in New York City. On the other hand, the South, despite its greater proximity to eastern financial centers, did not become part of the national capital market until the 1920s or 1930s.[42] An efficient market in the Pacific region and the lack of a regional market in the South may be the key to each case. Furthermore, the lack of a capital market in the South which could mobilize home savings and facilitate the inflows of outside savings may also help explain the level of stagnation experienced by the South through the early 1930s. Conversely, the Pacific Coast region may have been able to maintain its high per capita income levels, despite extraordinary in-migration of labor, because of the existence of a regional market capable of mobilizing capital to and in the region.

A model of regional financial market development and national market integration will be designed in Chapter 3 to provide a framework in which to investigate questions of regional growth under isolation, and issues of the process of national capital market formation. This framework will be applied to the economic history of the Pacific Coast region in subsequent chapters. The concluding chapter will use a comparison of the American South and the Pacific Coast region to form some conjectures about the causes of southern stagnation in the late nineteenth and early twentieth centuries.

NOTES

1. This abstracts from the possibility of disembodied technological change.
2. Raymond Goldsmith, *Financial Structure and Development* (New Haven: Yale University Press, 1969), 392.
3. This is the term employed by Lance Davis and Douglass North in *Institutional Change and American Economic Growth* (Cambridge: Cambridge University Press, 1971).
4. Douglas Dowd, "A Comparative Analysis of Economic Development in the American West and South," *Journal of Economic History* 16 (December 1956), 559.
5. John Gurley and Edward Shaw, "Financial Aspects of Economic Development," *American Economic Review* 45 (September 1955), 515-538.
6. Goldsmith, *Financial Structure and Development.*
7. Joseph Schumpeter, *The Theory of Economic Development* (Cambridge: Harvard University Press, 1934), 66.
8. Alexander Gerschenkron, *Economic Backwardness in Historical Perspective* (New York: Praeger, 1965); Rondo Cameron et al., *Banking in the Early States of Industrialization* (New York: Oxford University Press, 1967).
9. Nathaniel Leff, "Capital Markets in the Less Developed Countries: The Group Principle," in *Money and Finance in Economic Growth and Development*, ed. Ronald McKinnon (New York: Marcel Dekker, 1976); Naomi Lamoreaux, "Banks, Kinship, and Economic Development: The New England Case," *Journal of Economic History* 46 (September 1986), 647-667.
10. Ronald McKinnon, *Money and Capital in Economic Development* (Washington, D.C.: Brookings, 1973), 8.
11. Lance Davis, et al., *American Economic Growth: An Economist's History of the United States* (New York: Harper and Row, 1972), 34.
12. Susan Previant Lee and Peter Passell, *A New Economic View of American History* (New York: Norton, 1979), 269.
13. Davis et al., *American Economic Growth*, 282.
14. Harvey Perloff, et al., *Regions, Resources, and Economic Growth* (Baltimore: Johns Hopkins Press, 1960), 131.

15. U.S. Bureau of the Census, *Historical Statistics of the United States: Colonial Times to 1970* (Washington, D.C.: Government Printing Office, 1975), series F238-F241.
16. Richard Easterlin, "Regional Income Trends," in Robert Fogel and Stanley Engerman, eds., *The Reinterpretation of American Economic History* (New York: Harper and Row, 1971), 44-45.
17. U.S. Bureau of the Census, *Historical Statistics*, series X580-X581.
18. U.S. Bureau of the Census, *Historical Statistics*, series X879-X880.
19. Jeremy Atack, Fred Bateman, and Thomas Weiss, "Risk, the Rate of Return, and the Pattern of Investment in Nineteenth Century American Manufacturing," *Southern Economic Journal* 49 (July 1982), 153.
20. Robert Fogel and Jack Rutner, "The Efficiency Effects of Federal Land Policy, 1850-1900: A Report of Some Provisional Findings," in William Aydelotte et al., eds., *The Dimensions of Quantitative Research in History* (Princeton: Princeton University Press, 1972), 398.
21. August Lösch, *The Economics of Location* (New Haven: Yale University Press: 1954), 472-473. Here, for example, distance translates into unfamiliarity with the borrower or his production process, and into difficulty transmitting information.
22. McKinnon [*Money and Capital*, 8] calls these differentials "the brute fact of underdevelopment."
23. D.M. Frederiksen, "Mortgage Banking in America," *Journal of Political Economy* 2 (December 1893), 207-209.
24. R.M. Breckenridge, "Discount Rates in the United States," *Political Science Quarterly* 13 (March 1898), 126.
25. Breckenridge, "Discount Rates," 129-132.
26. Lance Davis, "The Investment Market, 1870-1914: The Evolution of a National Market," *Journal of Economic History* 25 (September 1965), 370.
27. Richard Sylla, "Federal Policy, Banking Market Structure, and Capital Mobilization in the United States, 1863-1913," *Journal of Economic History* 29 (December 1969), 664, 670.

28. John James, *Money and Capital Markets in Postbellum America* (Princeton: Princeton University Press, 1978).
29. Gene Smiley, "Interest Rate Movement in the United States, 1888-1913," *Journal of Economic History* 35 (September 1975), 595, 601, 607-609.
30. Hugh Rockoff, "Regional Interest Rates and Bank Failures, 1870-1914," *Explorations in Economic History* 14 (January 1977), 93.
31. Marie Sushka and Brian Barrett, "Banking Structure and the National Capital Market," *Journal of Economic History* 44 (June 1984), 463-477.
32. Barry Eichengreen, "Mortgage Rates in the Populist Era," *American Economic Review* 74 (December 1984), 995-1015.
33. Kenneth Snowden, "Mortgage Rates and American Capital Market Development in the Late Nineteenth Century," *Journal of Economic History* 47 (September 1987), 671-691.
34. Robert Sexton, "The Effect of Alternative Regional Delineations on Historical Interpretation," *Economic Forum* 12 (Winter 1981-1982), 78.
35. Jeffrey G. Williamson, "Antebellum Urbanization in the American Northeast," *Journal of Economic History* 25 (December 1965), 594.
36. For example, the mean of a normal distribution contains much more information about the distribution than the mean of a bi-modal distribution.
37. John James, "The Development of the National Money Market, 1893-1911," *Journal of Economic History* 36 (December 1976), 878; my emphasis.
38. Vincent Carosso, "Proposals for a Regional Financial History of the Middle Atlantic States," in *Regional Economic History: The Mid-Atlantic Area Since 1700*, ed. Glenn Porter (Wilmington, Delaware: Eleutherian Mills-Hagley Foundation, 1976).
39. Diane Lindstrom, *Economic Development in the Philadelphia Region, 1810-1850* (New York: Columbia University, Press, 1978).
40. Gavin Wright, *Old South, New South* (New York: Basic Books, 1986). See also Joshua Rosenbloom, "One Market or Many? Labor Market Integration in the Late Nineteenth-

Century United States," *Journal of Economic History* 50 (March 1990), 85-107, for an analysis of national labor market integration.

41. Work in this genre includes banking histories of states, and histories of individual financial institutions. Examples include early work by Lance Davis, and pieces by George Green, [*Finance and Economic Development in the Old South* (Stanford: Stanford University Press, 1972)], and Alan Olmstead, [*New York City Mutual Savings Banks, 1819-1861* (Chapel Hill: University of North Carolina Press, 1976)].
42. Davis, "The Investment Market," 388-389.

CHAPTER 3

Conceptualizing Regional Financial Markets

The failure to investigate financial market formation at a regional level has created a gap in economic historians' analysis of growth and development in the United States. Such regional markets play two crucial roles: they mobilize existing funds when connection to outside financial markets have yet to form, and they promote the attachment to a national market by reducing the costs of funds inflows. Individual analysis of the formation of these markets in different regions is essential, since the factors which underlie regional financial market development differ from place to place and period to period. The assumption that a regional market exists seems implicit in most histories of regional growth (which ignore the market issue) and is explicit in national financial market integration research. This assumption is rarely tested, and it limits the explanations for divergent regional growth patterns and for differing rates of attachment to a national financial market.

FINANCIAL MARKETS IN ISOLATED REGIONS

The extent of financial markets in an isolated region is crucial to the prospects of economic growth and development within that region. Consider an area which, due to geographical, technological, or social barriers, is limited in the resources it can exploit to those found within its own boundaries. There is a range of possible growth and production patterns available to the region, given its resources; these could be summarized in a production possibilities frontier. The maximum production levels on this frontier assume the ability to transfer natural resources, labor, and capital into their most profitable uses. If markets are not in place to coordinate production decisions with production opportunities across the region, resources will be used less efficiently and the economy will not attain an optimum point on the production possibilities frontier.

In particular, we can discuss the importance of markets for investable funds. The purpose of such markets is to coordinate the decisions of surplus units (savers) with deficit units (borrowers). For the most part, these units are not comprised of the same people: those who save are not necessary those with the talent to profitably use those savings. The larger is the region, and the more dispersed are saving accumulations and investment opportunities, the more important will be some market mechanism to transfer funds to the best investment project. The market should consist of an aggregation of information on the locations, amounts, and costs of savings within the region, and on the types, locations, and expected returns of investment opportunities. The centralization of this information allows both borrowers and lenders to survey, at relatively low cost, the possible sources and uses of funds available within the region. Information on the full distribution of returns available allows a rational and efficient employment of resources.

It is important that this market be centralized at some known point in the region. As Gras pointed out, "The storage of fluid capital is much the same as the storage of merchandise. It can best be done in the metropolitan centers and from there be taken out for use where and when desired."[1] Unlike merchandise, however, financial transactions involve the trade of money not for goods, but for the promise of money in the future. Consequently, the collection of information on the parties to the transaction and on the expected outcome of the transaction are more important in finance than in commerce. It is essential that the maximum amount of information be accumulated in one central location, from which all possible transactions may be investigated. The establishment of one city which acts as a clearinghouse for information and as a location for financial institutions in the region is crucial. Many smaller urban centers acting as localized financial centers improve funds flows only over the local area. Unless these cities are connected into a regional network or centralized market, the flow of funds on a regional scale will be impeded.

The consequences of market failure (or, more precisely, the failure of a market to form) for a region limited to indigenous savings are numerous. In such a circumstance, there are four options for the borrower wishing to finance an investment project. First, he can spend the time and effort required to canvass the entire region in search of the appropriate amount of savings at the lowest possible interest rate. The costs of this are extremely high, however, especially in large regions with disperse savings accumulations. Second, he can limit himself to search within the local area, thereby reducing his search costs but possibly paying a higher rate or failing to find sufficient funds. Third, he can self-finance the project, postponing investment and reducing consumption levels until he has accumulated sufficient personal savings to pay for the project. Finally, the potential investor may find it so difficult to obtain funds that he abandons the project altogether.

The saver, too, faces a similar number of options in a region without a financial market. He can, like the borrower, use part of his resources in searching for the best risk/return combination offered by a borrower in the region, or he can limit himself to projects within his locale. He may decide to invest the funds in his own project even if he has little expertise or expectation of return. Finally, he may accumulate the savings in an idle hoard, precluding any potential output the funds might have produced. Clearly, none of these outcomes is optimal if the objective of the residents in the region is to maximize economic growth and development subject to the fixed resource base. The wider the geographical and sectoral range of investment opportunities and the more disperse the savings accumulations, the more costly any personal or non-market search for sources or uses of funds. At some threshold, these costs will be so high that no investment projects will be funded, and no savings will be employed. The economy will be operating inside the production possibilities frontier.

REGIONAL MARKETS IN NATIONAL INTEGRATION

In addition to its impact on the efficient mobilization of indigenous savings, the existence of a regional financial market can play a crucial role in the linkage of a region to a national capital market. The magnitude of difficulty involved in transferring funds across regions is a multiple of that encountered in mobilizing funds within regions. The problems faced by outside savers are compounded by added distance (which increases transaction and monitoring costs) and by greater unfamiliarity with the region (which increases information costs and which may increase risk premiums).

If the region has developed an internal market for funds which revolves around a financial center having information and transaction links into the region, this network can be used by outside agents to place funds in the region. The market lowers the search and information costs which an outside saver would otherwise have faced. Consequently, the net return to the saver increases and the net cost to the borrower decreases, promoting the inflow of funds to the region. This is the beginning of national market integration.

Consider a symbolic representation of this problem. The costs of financial flows across a country comprised of a number of regions may be decomposed into interregional costs and intraregional costs. Interregional costs may be thought of as the costs of funds transfers between the major cities of two different regions. Intraregional costs, on the other hand, are the costs of transferring funds from a major city to a point in the regional hinterland of that city. Thus, the transfer of savings from a resident of New York City to a project in Seattle could be separated into the interregional cost between New York City and San Francisco, and the intraregional cost between San Francisco and Seattle.[2]

let C_1 = interregional cost of funds flow between New York City and San Francisco, faced by New Yorkers or San Franciscans

let C_2 = intraregional cost of funds flow between San Francisco and Seattle, faced by San Franciscans

let C_3 = intraregional cost of funds flow between San Francisco and Seattle, faced by New Yorkers

Isard and Tung have suggested that the amount of information on Seattle that a New York resident must explicitly collect is higher than the amount that a San Franciscan must collect. The San Francisco resident benefits from "high visibility" of activities and conditions within the region, and so has to put less information in explicit form.[3] That part of intraregional costs which results from transactions and monitoring will also be lower for the San Francisco resident, due to simple proximity advantages over the New Yorker. That is,

$$C_2 < C_3$$

and $[C_1 + C_2] < [C_1 + C_3]$

Thus, it would pay for a New York resident to use an agent in San Francisco who will transfer funds to Seattle, as long as the agent's fee is less than $[C_3 - C_2]$. This agent may be a resident of San Francisco whom the New York resident hires. This would involve the cost incurred in establishing the trustworthiness of the agent; in the past this cost was reduced by hiring local bankers or lawyers as financial agents. Or, the New Yorker could send a colleague from his own city to San Francisco to establish an agency. In this case, the riskiness of hiring an unknown San Francisco resident is avoided, but there is a cost involved in familiarizing the New York agent with his environment on the Pacific Coast. Clearly there is a trade-off in reducing risk versus reducing information costs. In either case, however, it is profitable for the New Yorker to maintain some sort of agent or intermediary in San Francisco, and the lower overall costs of lending achieved by an agency in San Francisco will promote funds flows between the regions.

An analogy may prove insightful here. Suppose there is a baseball game in which a fly ball hit to center field needs to be thrown to home plate in order to tag out a base runner. The outfielder, 350 feet away from home plate, will frequently throw the ball to an infielder who is positioned halfway between the outfielder and home plate. This infielder will relay the ball to home plate. The ultimate objective is to get the baseball from center field to home plate. By transferring the baseball by way of the infielder, however, the speed and accuracy of the throw can often be increased and the direction of the throw can be corrected if conditions warrant (such as if the base runner does not try to reach home plate or if another base runner tries to advance). If one thinks of the baseball as funds, the outfielder as a saver in New York City, and home plate as an investment project in Seattle, the analogy is clear. An intermediary in San Francisco who is closer to Seattle (and so has better "aim" with the funds) and who possesses superior information on the conditions surrounding the investment project ("home plate" and the other bases) can improve the speed and accuracy with which savings flow to their ultimate goal.

Of course, the New York City resident (the outfielder) could attempt to transfer the funds (the baseball) to Seattle (home plate) himself, but the speed of the funds flow may be so reduced as to miss the opportunity (tagging the runner). The costs of trying to transfer funds over such long distances may be so high that the transfer is not expected to have a positive net return. Consequently, while funds may flow in to a region which lacks financial intermediaries, the cost of these funds to local borrowers may be prohibitive and the responsiveness of funds inflows to new opportunities may be very slow.

The availability of agents in an urban center where financial information can be gathered thus speeds capital inflows by reducing the intraregional costs faced by an outside lender. If a formal financial market (such as a stock exchange or bank correspondent system) is in place in a region, moreover, the cost C_3 declines dramatically, and can even fall to near the level of C_2. Insofar as the outside resident can use the market institutions in place in the regional financial center, he also saves the costs of retaining an agent who must collect information in the urban center. Again, the total costs of national lending $[C_1 + C_3]$ are greatly reduced, and market integration can occur at a faster pace.

The decomposition of the financial flow process into two parts, interregional and intraregional, is quite useful. Now, the failure of a region to receive funds inflows can be seen as a function of two factors. First, distance and technology may be such that communication between regions is primitive, and interregional costs C_1 are high. This would prohibit inflows of funds to the major centers of regions. On the other hand, an area which is quite close to a lender region may be so poorly served by internal financial networks that the costs of transferring funds within the area (intraregional costs C_2) are prohibitive. It is the total cost $[C_1 + C_2]$ which will ultimately determine funds flows. The focus on C_1 alone, which appears to be the case in most capital market integration literature (if the costs are specified at all), and the failure to consider C_2 and C_3 limit explanations for why the South failed to integrate until the 1930s, while the Pacific Coast region appeared to integrate twenty to thirty years earlier.

FOUNDATIONS OF REGIONAL FINANCIAL MARKETS

Clearly, the extent to which a financial center forms within a region, and the depth of its network into the region, will determine both the ability to recycle home savings and the ability to attract and mobilize funds inflows. The key features of a region which appear to determine financial market development are the characteristics of commercial ties within the region. Finance follows commerce; Charles Kindleberger writes that "both banking and commerce involve the overcoming of distance, and the geographical pattern of banking was linked to commerce."[4] A region comprised of localized trade and scattered, small urban centers not connected by a metropolitan hierarchy will not have the potential for regional financial market formation. Thus, in studying the formation of regional financial markets, it is crucial to investigate regional commercial patterns.

Because finance involves the trade of current purchasing power for the promise of purchasing power to be returned in the future, there is a great deal of uncertainty involved in the transaction. As a result, financial flows depend upon careful accumulation and assessment of information. This point has been raised by economic geographers (most carefully by William Code) and by urban economists (such as Pred) who argue that the information flows within and between regions are critical in determining the flow of capital.[5] The agglomeration and analysis required of financial information is therefore key in mapping out the size of capital markets. The easier it is to accumulate, transfer, and evaluate information on investment opportunities, the easier it is for financial connections to stretch from investments to savers some distance away. Conversely, the more difficult it is to collect and assess information, the more likely it is that investors will have to depend on capital closer to home. Thus, there is an implicit regionality in capital markets, defined by the location of investments and savings, and by the patterns of information flows.

The importance of information flow patterns can be combined with notions of commercial networks and merchant profits to build a framework for studying the development of regional financial markets. It is generally agreed that mercantile profits represent the earliest source of investable funds in developing economies.[6] It is fortunate that this supply of funds resides in the pockets of merchants; these businessmen are likely to seek out new investment projects within the region. Merchants in newly developing regions have also been seen as less risk-averse than other early immigrants who settle in a new region and begin as subsistence producers.[7] Consequently, merchants may be more willing to place their savings in the high risk ventures which characterize new settlements. The financial role of merchants may also become so prominent that we find them specializing in the "financial side of commerce."[8] For example, in the United States, merchants' habit of endorsing their customers' loans regularly evolved into the establishment of merchant banks.

In addition to accumulated savings funds and lower risk aversion, merchants benefit from owning the most liquid resources in a new community--cash and inventories. Gurley and Shaw show theoretically that the desire for portfolio diversification and liquidity limits the amount of illiquid direct debt that a saver is willing to hold.[9] In a new region which lacks financial intermediaries, all debt is direct debt. Merchants, then, be more willing to carry long-term illiquid debt from investors than will farmers or manufacturers who hold a great deal of fixed, illiquid assets such as land or plant and equipment.

Merchants, then, have the willingness and the ability to invest in a new region. They also have access to the information required to evaluate investment projects in the region. Merchants naturally gather information on production opportunities in the process of buying from producers and wholesalers and selling to retailers and customers. The shifting regional demands for export goods, import-substituting goods, residentiary goods and services, and infrastructure are evident first to the middlemen who make the market--the merchants. Estimates of creditworthiness are also a natural adjunct of commerce. These types of information are exactly what is required by the potential lender.[10] Merchant finance in most developing countries exhibits a natural progression from investment in export goods, to investment in infrastructure needed to market those goods, production of import-substituting goods for residents, and finally to residentiary and footloose industries.

Where merchants gather, there is a savings supply and an information accumulation. Both of these are necessary conditions for the development of a financial center which can anchor a regional market. Merchants tend to cluster at entrepôt cities--cities located at transportation hubs along commercial networks, where goods are processed and/or warehoused. The larger the hinterland served commercially by this entrepôt city, the greater the city's potential as a financial center. While commercial transactions and production may take place at many locations throughout a region, it is crucial that the inflow of financial information be centralized as much as possible. The uncertainty of finance places a premium on face-to-face contact[11] and on maximum information regarding the parties to the transaction. Consequently, the more centralized is the financial market within a region, the more uncertainty will be reduced.[12]

A region which has a centralized commercial market with well-developed links throughout the hinterland will have a foundation for an efficient regional financial market. This market, centered on a financial metropolis, can act as an intermediary for savers in the metropolis, in the regional hinterland, and also outside the region. Conversely, a region where production is very localized and merchants are scattered in many small and unrelated urban centers is not a favorable environment for regional financial market formation. The mercantile profits are likely to be small, and there will not be a single entrepôt in which merchants gather. Neither financial information nor investable savings will accumulate in a centralized location. The probable result is localized finance, in which the regional distribution of investment returns and costs remain hidden to lenders and borrowers. Clearly, this is not optimal.

LINEAR MODELS AND NODAL MODELS OF FINANCE

This conceptualization of financial development is a reaction to what may be termed a "linear" model of such development. Certainly, the failure to investigate regional financial market formation may be only an oversight on the part of economic historians who are addressing broader issues. On the other hand, the emphasis on attachment to a national financial center in New York City may stem from a more serious misconception. The researchers may subscribe to a model in which underdeveloped areas are presumed to wait in isolated ignorance until the westward and southward push of excess funds and financiers from New York reaches their borders.

It is argued here that finance naturally develops first on a local scale (as does commerce) unless there are barriers to such development; these barriers must be specified. When local outlets for residents' savings are exhausted, the lender may begin to search outside his locale, usually in an area with the lowest transactions costs, such as a city. Similarly, when local sources of funds are exhausted, the borrower will search outside his area, in low cost centers such as cities. There is, from the point of view of lenders and borrowers, an outward push of financial connections; the development of financial ties does not logically begin on an interregional scale.

The entrance of a lender from New York City into the southern or western United States, or the search in New York City for funds by borrowers from these regions, should occur after regional market opportunities have been exhausted. The exact timing of outside search (and the beginning of national market integration) depends both upon the relative demands for and supplies of funds in a region, and on the costs of search inside and outside the region. The less developed is the internal market, the more costly it is for lenders to pursue opportunities there, and the longer it will take to achieve market connection, ceteris paribus. Of course, funds may flow into regions without internal markets, but the cost will be high, and large interest differentials will exist. Furthermore, the coordination of investment opportunities and funds inflow will be poor, and interest rate movement in the areas will not be highly correlated.[13] It is also possible for borrowers to quickly exhaust possibilities at home, because of scarce savings, or high risk premiums or transactions costs. They may search outside the area for funds at a point early in the development of the region, but the search is likely to result in large interest differentials and low interest rate correlation.[14]

What is termed the "linear" model of market development in the United States focuses on the role of eastern lenders in creating markets as excess savings push connections westward and southward; it is the model implicit in previous research on national capital market integration. This model also emphasizes the advantages of sophisticated financial development or scale economies which benefit eastern lenders. On the other hand, the "nodal" model of market development offered here emphasizes the role of local lenders and borrowers in newly developing regions, and the locational advantages of regional financial connections. In this model, a region's residents do not necessarily sit idle and forego local investment opportunities while waiting for capital from the East. Instead, regional connections are formed to an extent dependent upon factors such as the level and dispersion of regional savings, and the depth of commercial networks, as discussed earlier. These regional markets can speed integration to the national financial center. Whether residents must wait for a linear financial push from the East or are able to attract eastern funds to a internal financial center (as in the nodal model) depends on the precursors to regional market formation. The nodal model, in which both intraregional and interregional costs are considered, is a more complete model of financial development than has been used by economic historians in the past. It provides a framework for the study of the Pacific Coast region in the late nineteenth and early twentieth centuries.

NOTES

1. N.S.B. Gras, *An Introduction to Economic History* (New York: Harper and Brothers, 1922), 255.
2. Robert Fogel, ["Railroads and American Economic Growth," in Robert Fogel and Stanley Engerman, eds., *The Reinterpretation of American Economic History* (New York: Harper & Row, 1971), 188-191] uses a similar distinction in his analysis of transportation costs; he separates the east-west (interregional) cost of transporting farm products from the cost of transporting products from the farm to nearby distribution centers (intraregional costs). Authors in the field of financial market integration have usually aggregated the two costs.
3. Walter Isard and Tze Hsiung Tung, "Some Concepts for the Analysis of Spatial Organization," *Papers and Proceedings of the Regional Science Association* 11 (1963), 36.
4. Charles Kindleberger, *Economic Response* (Cambridge: Harvard University Press, 1978), 72-73.
5. William R. Code, "The Spatial Dynamics of Financial Intermediaries: An Interpretation of the Distribution of Financial Decision-Making in Canada" (Ph.D. diss., University of California, 1971); Allan Pred, *The Spatial Dynamics of U.S. Urban-Industrial Growth, 1800-1914* (Cambridge: MIT Press, 1966).
6. See Glenn Porter and Harold Livesay, *Merchants and Manufacturers* (Baltimore: Johns Hopkins Press, 1971) and Elisha Douglass, *The Coming of Age of American Business* (Chapel Hill: University of North Carolina Press, 1971) for forceful accounts of the role of merchants in economic structure and growth. An example of a study of merchants in the antebellum period is found in Arthur Johnson and Barry Supple, *Boston Capitalists and Western Railroads* (Cambridge: Harvard University Press, 1967).
7. See Porter and Livesay, *Merchants and Manufacturers* and Thomas Senior Berry, *Early California: Gold, Prices, Trade* (Richmond, Virginia: The Bostwick Press, 1984) for accounts of the risk encountered by merchants in new regions.

8. Charles Kindleberger finds exactly the same patterns in merchant behavior in developing England. Kindleberger, *Economic Response*, 72.
9. Gurley and Shaw, "Financial Aspects," 525.
10. James Madison, ["The Evolution of Commercial Credit Reporting Agencies in Nineteenth-Century America," *Business History Review* 48 (Summer 1974)] discusses the formalization of 19th century mercantile information networks by the Bradstreet and Dun commercial reporting agencies; these reports have a clear financial application.
11. See Sidney Robbins and Nestor Terleckyj, *Money Metropolis* (Cambridge: Harvard University Press, 1960), 33-34.
12. Working against the tendency to centralize are the costs of explicit information collection, information transmission costs, and transactions and monitoring costs which increase with distance from the investment project. The unfamiliarity with new regions and the primitive nature of communication between older and newer regions discourages the immediate formation of a highly centralized national market.
13. Of course, the magnitude of the interregional barriers or costs also determines interest differentials and correlations. The higher these barriers, the larger interest differentials, and the lower rate correlations.
14. The borrower's search may be complicated by capital flight from the developing region. If internal markets are very underdeveloped, savers may prefer to place funds in a more developed region, at low or zero return, rather than lend through unreliable or costly channels. See Harry W. Richardson, *Regional Growth Theory* (New York: John Wiley and Sons, 1973) and Gunnar Myrdal, *Economic Theory and Under-Developed Regions* (London: Duckworth, 1957) for discussions of this "uphill flow" of funds in less developed countries.

CHAPTER 4

Capital and Growth in the Pacific Region

THE EARLY PACIFIC COAST REGION

By the middle of the nineteenth century, the United States had officially extended her boundaries to the Pacific Ocean. In 1846, the Oregon Compromise, (a treaty with Great Britain), added 285,580 square miles to the country, an area stretching from the Continental Divide in the east to the Pacific Ocean in the west, and bounded by the 42nd parallel in the south and the 49th parallel in the north. It included the current states of Oregon, Washington, Idaho, and portions of Montana and Wyoming. The Mexican Cession of February 1848 increased American territory by another 529,017 square miles, including the land now covered by California, Nevada, Utah, and portions of Arizona, New Mexico, and Colorado. What were to be the three most populous of these western states--California, Oregon, and Washington--were admitted to the Union in 1850, 1859, and 1889, respectively.[1]

The addition of these territories to the United States was accomplished without great expense or bloodshed. Both the Oregon Compromise and the Mexican Cession were, more or less, simple recognitions of increasing American settlement in these areas, and of the power of Manifest Destiny to carve out a contiguous nation on the North American continent. Neither Great Britain nor Mexico could have foreseen the vast riches to be produced by these territories. In fact, the primitive nature of communication which had been a factor in Mexico's difficulty ruling "Alta California" and in its subsequent willingness to cede the area, turned out to produce an American claim on an even greater prize than could have been imagined. On January 24, 1848, nine days before the Treaty of Guadalupe Hidalgo was signed ceding the territory to the United States (too short a period to transmit much accurate information from the Californian hinterland), gold was discovered at Sutter's mill near present-day Sacramento. Although the gold production of California was certainly an early impetus to her settlement and to the economic development of the Pacific Coast, the area developed a vibrant and diversified economy by the 1870s which had little to do with the mineral stocks of the region.

Prior to annexation in the 1840s, American settlements and economic activity dotted the coastline of the Pacific Ocean. The earliest commercial activity in the Pacific Northwest began in the late eighteenth century when Americans, British, and Russians discovered the potential for trapping beaver and otter in the area.[2] The Northwest Company and her successor the Hudson's Bay Company (formed in 1821) were leaders in the fur trade of the Pacific Northwest's interior; Hudson's Bay Company established its headquarters at Fort Vancouver, near present-day Portland, Oregon, in 1824. This company expanded its activities to include merchant and factor services for settlers in the Willamette Valley of Oregon who were engaged in agricultural production, largely of wheat for subsistence and for sale in limited markets in England and Hawaii. The Company had a virtual monopoly on the sale of supplies and the purchase of agricultural output in this area; this may have constrained economic growth and settlement. The monopoly went so far as to prohibit the sale of cattle to settlers; the Company would rent animals, but not allow settlers to develop independent herds through breeding.[3]

Hudson's Bay Company also created an independent Puget Sound Agricultural Company in Washington state; the first major settlement in this vicinity appeared on Puget Sound in 1845 with the establishment of the town of Tumwater. Washington had lagged considerably behind Oregon in settlement activity and agricultural development. While the Willamette and Columbia rivers in Oregon allowed agricultural products to reach the sea, there was no similar confluence of rivers in Washington. Consequently, the amount of arable land which had access to shipping routes was limited to the edges of Puget Sound. In sum, the majority of commercial activity in the Pacific Northwest before the mid-1840s was funded and controlled by the Hudson's Bay Company; urban settlements were few and small.[4]

During the pre-gold rush period in California, no company such as Hudson's Bay dominated economic life, but the area was not one of great population growth and economic activity either. The original pattern of settlement and production was created in the missions of the Catholic Church, where Indian labor was used to produce a variety of agricultural goods such as wheat, grapes, and citrus fruits. With independence from Spain in 1821, Mexico secularized the missions and began its policy of granting choice tracts of land to favored citizens. By the mid-1840s, these grants totalled nearly eight million acres, located mostly along the coast or in the Sacramento River valley. The ranchos on these lands were principally involved in cattle ranching and the production of tallow and hides, which were shipped from the coast to the boot and shoe industry in New England. The earliest immigrants into California in the 1830s usually assumed the role of merchant, facilitating the trade in hides and tallow and the import of luxury goods for the landed classes. The cities of San Francisco (then called Yerba Buena) and Los Angeles were established around the early missions in the 1770s, and grew to be minor pueblos servicing the trade in hides, tallow, and fur in the 1830s.

MINERAL WEALTH IN THE PACIFIC COAST REGION

The entire Pacific Coast region on the eve of its annexation, and, more importantly, on the eve of the California gold rush, was characterized by limited and scattered settlement, and the production of agricultural products for limited export trade. In other words, the area was a typical frontier region. The discovery of gold in the Sierra Nevada foothills in 1848 altered that status quickly, dramatically, and permanently. The gold that flowed out of California mines laid the foundation for a strong regional economy in the Pacific Coast region, centered on the metropolis of San Francisco. The gold rush attracted the initial large immigration to the region and spurred investment both in the production of capital goods to support the gold mining industry, and in the production of consumer goods to support the newly burgeoning population. The gold rush also had the unique effect of providing an immediately saleable commodity with a worldwide market and universal liquidity.[5]

Furthermore, the fact that the minerals taken from Sierra mines were owned by residents of the region, not by absentee investors, meant that a large new supply of home-owned savings was available which could finance the continuing development of the region. The geography of the Pacific Coast region and the unique location and timing of the gold rush resulted in the commercial primacy of San Francisco and in its eventual financial dominance of the region. Jane Jacobs comments that "when the discovery of gold in California resulted in the formation of San Francisco in 1849, it behaved like the cities of Europe and the U.S. North. Loosely speaking, it played the economic role of Venice in the Far West, much as Boston and Philadelphia had played that role in the East."[6] Instead of separate, isolated, outward-looking relationships to other countries or to the eastern United States, the Pacific Coast states, under the leadership of California and San Francisco, forged an integrated regional economy where internal relationships were as important or more important than ties with the outside world. The pace and progress of the region was not limited or circumscribed by a long sojourn in the "colonial" stage. San Francisco and California seemed to skip this stage entirely and claimed the Pacific Northwest for their own economic hinterland.

It took several months for the news of the gold rush to reach the outside world and, more importantly, for it to be confirmed. As Bean points out, "There had been idle rumors of gold ever since the expeditions of Drake and Vizcaino."[7] Mention was made of the discovery in two San Francisco weekly newspapers in March 1848, but the "fever did not begin to be epidemic" until a merchant at Sutter's Fort, Samuel Brannan, noticed that many traders were paying for his goods with gold. After having bought up all the available merchandise in Northern California which gold miners might need, Brannan visited San Francisco on May 12, and walked the streets waving a bottle of gold dust and announcing the event. He was a shrewd businessman, because his dramatics set off a huge migration of Californians to the Sierras.

Samples of the gold were sent to the provisional capital at Monterey, and these were passed on to Washington D.C. In his December message to Congress, President Polk used the gold discovery as justification for his policies which led to the Mexican Cession.[8] The veins of gold subsequently ceded to the United States were rich indeed. Berry estimates that in 1848, the mint value of California gold production equalled $5,695,000. This figure increased sharply to $53,021,000 in 1850, and hit a peak in 1852 with $66,640,000 in gold taken from the California mines.[9] Berry's figures total $641,117,000 in gold mined between 1848 and 1860. From 1848 to 1948, a total of approximately 2 billion dollars in gold was mined in California.[10]

While the Sierra gold mines had passed their peak production in the early 1850s, the discovery of western Nevada's tremendous Comstock Lode of silver (and minor amounts of gold) set off a new mining boom between 1859 and 1864. A further upsurge in 1867 peaked by 1875; a total of 400 million dollars in silver and gold was mined from the Comstock before it played out in the early 1880s.[11] California's good fortune in finding precious metals (the Comstock mines were largely owned by Californians) was unparalleled in the United States, but the Pacific Northwest also contained rich deposits of precious metals. The most significant of these were in the Oro Fino, Florence, Boise Basin, and Owyhee districts of eastern Oregon Territory. Between 1858 and 1867, the value of mining production in Washington, Oregon, and Idaho totalled 75 million dollars.[12] These totals, though far below those of California, were significant in attracting settlers.

Following in this vein, it must be reiterated that while the tremendous mineral riches of the Pacific Coast region in general, and of California in particular, first brought the region to national attention, attracted labor and provided wealth, the long run growth and development of the region depended upon other types of productive activity. The California gold rush did forge strong and lasting ties among the states of the region and created the foundation for a vibrant regional economy. Over time, however, the progress of this economy was largely independent of the mining sector, and prospered despite isolation from the population centers of the United States.

DIVERSIFICATION OF THE PACIFIC COAST ECONOMY

Agricultural and natural resource industries, which had their beginnings in demand engendered by the mining industry in California, grew to be the leading industries of the Pacific Northwest through the 1920s. "(T)he sudden creation of this large external market [California] with its highly inflationary impact on prices of wheat and lumber, broke down the barriers which had circumscribed the development of the Oregon Country and gave impetus to investment in agriculture, the lumber industry, transportation, and construction."[13] Not only were hundreds of thousands of new settlers lured into the Pacific region,[14] (many with the intention of making quick profits and then returning to the East), but the demands of a huge new labor force on the coast opened up possibilities for profits in the production of goods to support the new industries and their labor force.[15] At first, the need was greatest for food and shelter, since the early capital requirements for placer mining (mining from riverbeds) were quite low. As a result, there arose a large and profitable trade in wheat and lumber from Oregon, and lumber from the Puget Sound area of Washington.[16] Gilbert estimates that prices of export staples from Oregon were 200 to 300 percent higher for three years after the gold rush than they had been before the rush began.[17] Thus, while the gold rush had drawn away much of the existing labor force of the Pacific Northwest, the return of satisfied (or, more often, disappointed) miners and the inflow of new settlers swelled the population, as can be seen in Table 4.1.[18]

Statistics on production in the Pacific Northwest states reflect the expansion of the labor supply and of a commercial market in the mid-1850s. Tattersall estimates that, in response to the enlarged demand coming from Pacific Coast residents, wheat production in the Pacific Northwest rose from 0.2 million bushels in 1850 to 2.6 million bushels in 1870, and 16.8 million bushels in 1890. The value of Oregon flour production rose from 1.2 million dollars in 1860 to 4.2 million dollars in 1890, while the value of Pacific Northwest lumber production rose from 1.9 million dollars in 1860 to 21.1 million dollars in 1890.[19] Table 4.2 shows that acreage in farms also increased dramatically, as did investment in farm implements, as is shown in Table 4.3. This is particularly true in Oregon where transportation on the Columbia and Willamette rivers opened profitable agricultural production for the California trade. Before the arrival of inland railroad transport in the 1880s, Washington concentrated on felling timber along the coastline of Puget Sound. These export staples of wheat, flour, and lumber which had found their initial market in California continued to dominate the economies of the Pacific

TABLE 4.1

PACIFIC COAST REGION POPULATION, 1850–1920

	California	Oregon	Washington
1850	93,000	12,000	1,000
1860	380,000	52,000	12,000
1870	560,000	91,000	24,000
1880	865,000	175,000	75,000
1890	1,213,000	318,000	357,000
1900	1,485,000	414,000	518,000
1910	2,378,000	673,000	1,142,000
1920	3,427,000	783,000	1,357,000

NOTES: Data from U.S. Bureau of the Census, *Historical Statistics of the United States: Colonial Times to 1970* (Washington, D.C.: Government Printing Office, 1975), Series A195.

TABLE 4.2

TOTAL FARM ACREAGE IN THE PACIFIC COAST REGION, 1850–1920

	California	Oregon	Washington
1850	3,894,000	433,000	na
1860	8,730,000	2,061,000	366,000
1870	11,427,000	2,389,000	649,000
1880	16,594,000	4,215,000	1,049,000
1890	21,427,000	6,910,000	4,179,000
1900	28,829,000	10,071,000	8,499,000
1910	27,931,000	11,685,000	11,712,000
1920	29,366,000	13,542,000	13,245,000

NOTES: Data from *Historical Statistics of the United States*, Series K77 to K79.

TABLE 4.3

TOTAL VALUE OF FARM MACHINERY, 1850–1920

	California	Oregon	Washington
1850	$ 103,483	$ 183,423	$ na
1860	2,558,506	952,313	190,402
1870	5,316,690	1,293,717	280,551
1880	8,447,744	2,956,173	958,513
1890	14,689,710	4,556,770	3,150,200
1900	21,311,670	6,506,725	6,271,630
1910	36,493,158	13,205,645	16,709,844
1920	136,069,290	41,567,125	54,721,377

NOTES: Data from 1900 U.S. Census, volume 5, pt. 1: *Agriculture*, 698; and 1920 U.S. Census, volume 5, pt. 1: *Agriculture*, 49.

Northwest through 1920, although diversification into other agricultural, extractive, and manufacturing industries occurred early in the twentieth century.[20]

Meanwhile, California sent a steady supply of gold to the Pacific Northwest in payment for wheat, lumber, and agricultural products, providing the first metallic medium of exchange in the region. But not all of California's population was engaged in gold mining. The lull in gold mining in the mid-1850s had created a mild depression in California, and the replacement of gold production with alternative activities was slow during this period. Cattle ranching continued to be an important holdover from the days of Mexican rule, but agriculture was hampered by unfamiliarity with California's dry climate, and by the insecurity of land titles in the state.[21]

In 1851, an Act of Congress sponsored by Senator William Gwin (said to be a spokesman for settlers in California) provided for the establishment of a board which was to decide the validity of all Mexican land grant titles. The average length of time required to establish ownership with these boards was seventeen years.[22] Since nearly all land grants had been in fertile agricultural areas, the tying up of these thirteen million acres in litigation was a significant barrier to the development of agriculture in the state until the last case was adjudicated in the 1860s. However, the availability of agricultural products from the Pacific Northwest via the coastal route freed Californian labor for other uses such as the manufacture of mining equipment and of saddlery (using the abundant cowhides).

While California's demand for lumber and wheat gave these industries their start in the Pacific Northwest, California soon developed her own agricultural and forestry base; according to Tattersall, however, San Francisco was still the best market for Pacific Northwest lumber in the 1880s.[23] In fact, the coast lumber trade to California equalled 200 million board feet in 1883-1884 and 323.6 million board feet in 1889.[24] California developed its redwood resources in the coast counties of Mendocino, Humboldt, and Santa Cruz, for a total production of 75 million board feet as early as 1860.[25] California also became a net wheat exporter by 1860, after the droughts of 1862-1864 had nearly wiped out the cattle ranching industry. Wheat was California's largest and most profitable agricultural commodity between the early 1860s and the depression of the early 1890s, when the industry collapsed due to competition from alternative producers in the United States and abroad.[26] The opening of the transcontinental railroad in the late 1860s and the spread of irrigated farming in the 1870s transformed California's agricultural base into one specialized in the production of fruits, vegetables, and assorted grains by the 1880s.

Estimates of the capital absorbed by manufacturing and processing industries was collected in the United States Censuses. Manufacturing appeared in the Pacific Northwest as early as the 1850s; by 1850, Oregon Territory had manufacturing establishments with total capital of $843,600 and product value of $2,236,640. Lumber sawmills, flour and grist mills, and woolen mills in the Northwest processed the abundant stocks of wheat, timber, and wool produced in Oregon and Washington. The manufacturing census figures show that between 1880 and 1920, lumber and timber products and flour and grist mill products were represented in the top three manufacturing industries of Oregon and Washington, by value of products.

California, unsurprisingly, had the early lead in manufacturing. By 1850, $1,006,197 was invested in manufacturing establishments which produced $12,862,522 worth of products. Sugar and molasses refining, using both California sugar beets and Hawaiian cane sugar (trade to Hawaii had opened by 1847), slaughtering, and flour and grist mill products dominated the value of production through 1900. In the early twentieth century, oil refineries, and canning and preserving plants arose to accommodate the newly discovered and/or newly profitable bases in petroleum and in irrigated farming. Throughout the period, the production of residentiary goods such as saddlery, and the production of machinery for mines and factories were important, thanks largely to the protective barrier of distance from eastern industrial giants.[27]

CREATING A REGIONAL ECONOMY

The forging of a regional economy would, of course, have been impossible without a transportation network linking the states and facilitating the specialization in and trade of goods. Until the 1880s, waterways provided the chief routes of commerce within the states of the region, and the coastal waterways sped commercial flows between the states. The Sacramento and San Joaquin Rivers of California's Central Valley opened into the excellent natural harbor of San

Francisco Bay, allowing easy ocean access for the agricultural hinterland of the state. The Willamette and Columbia Rivers made possible the shipment of Oregon wheat from the hinterland to San Francisco; timber from the shores of Puget Sound in Washington was easily transported south.[28] California's internal waterways were dominated by the California Steam Navigation Company, which had absorbed most competitors on the rivers by 1854. River traffic in Oregon had been monopolized early in the century by the Hudson's Bay Company; in the 1860s, the Portland-based Oregon Steam Navigation Company dominated the routes.

Although a rail line from Portland to San Francisco was anticipated in the 1860s and two firms incorporated to build such a line in 1866, the connection was not completed until 1887. This was long after the transcontinental railroad had been completed to San Francisco in 1869, and after Portland had been reached in 1883 and the direct line to Tacoma, Washington had been finished in 1887.[29] The lack of a rail connection between San Francisco and the Pacific Northwest is not a reflection of the lack of commerce between the points, but of the overwhelming advantage of shipping via established water routes. The delayed rail connections of Oregon and Washington to the east strengthened San Francisco's commercial dominance of those states, since goods shipped by rail had to pass first through that city.[30]

The fact that the first transcontinental railway, completed in 1869, had its terminus in San Francisco is not surprising.[31] The earliest plans for a railway to cross the nation were drawn in the 1840s and envisioned a route terminating in Oregon, but the discovery of gold in California and the headlong rush to that area changed those plans.[32] The railway completed to San Francisco was both a reflection of that city's predominance on the Pacific Coast and a means by which that dominance was maintained until northern routes were completed in the mid-1880s. By that time, however, many trade and service relationships had been cemented between San Francisco and the rest of the Pacific Coast region, so that the city easily dominated other transcontinental termini such as Portland, Tacoma, and Seattle.[33]

This dominance of a singe urban center is crucial in the formation of a regional financial market, as Chapter 3 has discussed.[34] The geographical configuration of the Pacific Coast plus the circumstance of the gold rush combined to assure that San Francisco would be the commercial and financial center of the West. The San Francisco Bay is deep, sheltered, and well connected to the interior of

California through the Sacramento and San Joaquin River systems. In California, Los Angeles had no natural harbor of equal size and quality. Although Portland had access to the "Inland Empire" of eastern Oregon and Washington and western Idaho via the Columbia River, the city was one hundred miles from the ocean and faced a difficult barrier of shifting sand bars. In Washington, Puget Sound had been described as a "harbor without a hinterland"[35] because the Cascade Mountains block the way between this natural harbor and the hinterland it might have served. Expenditures on river improvements and railways in the 1880s and 1890s would open up opportunities for ports on the Sound, but, again, San Francisco had gained the initial advantage which was nearly insurmountable through the early 1900s.[36] Consequently, in 1880, population in San Francisco exceeded 233,000, while Los Angeles contained little more than 11,000 residents, Portland had under 18,000, and Seattle had only 3,500 citizens.[37]

PACIFIC COAST ISOLATION

Prior to the completion of the transcontinental railroad to San Francisco in 1869, passage between the eastern United States and the Pacific Coast was extraordinarily slow and cumbersome. The average sailing time between San Francisco and New York City was 150 days in the late 1840s, due largely to delays at Panama. This was reduced to 89 days with the advent of the clipper ships in 1851.[38] The time required for passage by overland stage was somewhat shorter at 60 days,[39] but this form of transportation was very limited in the type and quantity of goods which could be carried. Delays of two to three months in the shipment of eastern goods (to meet constantly shifting demands in the region) gave the Pacific Coast a certain amount of "natural tariff" protection.

Consequently, residents had the opportunity to develop import-substituting infant industries which otherwise might have been out-competed by established eastern producers, as they had been in the American South and Midwest. Of course, the completion of the railroad in 1869 opened up the Pacific market to eastern goods, especially those from Chicago merchants whose warehouses lay at the terminus of the line.[40] By this time, however, the Pacific Coast region had twenty years of isolation in which to develop a certain industrial base.[41]

> Overnight a large population had gathered in a frontier, isolated state, and the presence of this population, so plentifully supplied with purchasing power, created an enormous market for goods and services of all kinds. The factors of time and distance were such, furthermore, as to overcome the disadvantages and handicaps of industrial and agricultural production in a frontier area. Miners needed tools, supplies, food, lumber, transportation facilities, wagons, leather; in fact, there was hardly anything they didn't need and couldn't pay for.[42]

What makes San Francisco and its role as urban center for the Pacific Coast region unique is that the city quickly became not only the commercial metropolis, but also the financial service center of the region, all within ten or twenty years of California's annexation in 1848. The San Francisco metropolitan area skipped, or passed very rapidly through, the lower stages of urban development and quickly became a service center, "exporting" commercial and financial services to the rest of the region.[43] Vance claims that only Boston, Philadelphia, and New York City had financial districts as specialized as San Francisco's in 1850.[44] The factors responsible for the appearance of a sophisticated financial center in a "frontier" region were the conjunction of wealth and isolation. Without the original accumulation of gold and gold rush-generated commercial wealth concentrated in San Francisco,[45] the region would probably have passed through the development process more slowly, as small accumulations of savings were self-invested or transferred only within the local area. In fact, large amounts of savings, from highly profitable industry and a young labor force, were accumulated in the commercial center of San Francisco, and were recycled throughout the region.

Without some degree of isolation from the rest of the country, it is likely that the function of financial intermediary would have been assumed by an established financial center such as New York City. Each area of the Pacific Coast region would then find it necessary to look to the East for investment funds and financial advice, with the possible consequence that Pacific Coast savings would be drained out and not re-invested at home.[46] With some degree of isolation, however, San Francisco was protected from competition in the financial sector as she was in the commercial sector. As a result, an in-region financial giant arose in the city, to recycle home savings throughout the Pacific Coast region.

It is clearly not true that eastern goods and eastern capital never flowed into the Pacific Coast region; some export goods industries such as minerals and timber did obtain funding in the East and in Europe. Nor is it true that local projects were never financed by capitalists scattered across the region or by the inflow of wealth carried by migrants themselves. It is true, however, that for the broad spectrum of investment needs and consumer goods, the states of the Pacific Coast region seemed to have relied on San Francisco. When San Francisco was not the ultimate source of the wealth invested, the city was the intermediary used to channel savings from other areas into Coast projects. San Francisco's superior information base made the city the clear choice for location of financiers and financial institutions. That is, "some 'intelligent' money was forthcoming from the East and Europe, but it was difficult to acquire without the approval of the financial community of San Francisco."[47]

CAPITAL IN THE PACIFIC COAST REGION

The quantities of capital investment and savings in the Pacific Coast region give an idea of the magnitude of the "financial problem" in the area. Tables 4.3 and 4.4 illustrate the rapid growth of investment in agriculture, manufacturing, and extractive and processing industries. The following brief sketches of leading industrial and agricultural sectors in the states should provide an idea of the types and amounts of capital required to support the development of these sectors.

TABLE 4.4

VALUE OF PRODUCTION AND CAPITAL INVESTED IN TOP FIVE MANUFACTURING SECTORS IN PACIFIC STATES, 1860–1919

	Industry	Aggregate Value of Products	Aggregate Value of Capital
CALIFORNIA			
1860	Gold Mining	$44,717,333	$11,005,876
	Flour and Meal	4,620,952	1,433,500
	Lumber, sawed	3,943,881	1,922,977
	Sugar, refined	1,586,500	300,000
	Machinery, Steam Engines,etc.	1,575,500	752,500
1870	Flouring and Grist Mill Products	9,036,386	2,590,400
	Lumber, sawed	5,227,064	3,856,440
	Molasses and Sugar, refined	3,904,045	1,300,000
	Quartz, milled	3,405,778	1,749,272
	Boots and shoes	2,214,807	489,854
1880	Flouring and Grist Mill Products	12,701,477	4,363,285
	Slaughtering	7,953,914	2,130,000
	Molasses and Sugar, refined	5,932,000	1,600,000
	Foundry and Machine Shop Products	4,797,232	3,040,189
	Boots and Shoes	4,581,099	1,296,685

TABLE 4.4
(continued)

	Industry	Aggregate Value of Products	Aggregate Value of Capital
CALIFORNIA			
1890	Molasses and Sugar Refining	$22,673,850	$5,509,965
	Flouring and Grist Mill Products	14,200,320	6,126,305
	Slaughtering and Meat Packing	9,768,858	2,220,536
	Lumber and Timber Products	8,794,655	16,184,235
	Foundry and Machine Shop Products	7,767,780	5,841,098
1900	Molasses and Sugar Refining	15,909,998	5,526,682
	Slaughtering	15,717,712	3,913,081
	Lumber and Timber	13,764,647	28,236,332
	Flour and Grist Mill Products	13,100,944	6,552,642
	Fruit and Vegetable, Preserve and Can	13,081,829	4,397,935
1909	Lumber and Timber Products	45,000,000	55,165,260
	Slaughtering and Meat Packing	34,280,000	11,463,407
	Fruit and Vegetable, Preserve and Can	32,915,000	18,316,474
	Foundry and Machine Shop Products	26,731,000	28,693,493
	Flour and Grist Mill Products	25,188,000	13,423,522

TABLE 4.4
(continued)

	Industry	Aggregate Value of Products	Aggregate Value of Capital
CALIFORNIA			
1919	Petroleum Refining	$213,292,000	$84,015,443
	Fruit and Vegetable, Preserve and Can	189,956,000	63,649,112
	Ship building, steel	179,152,000	108,798,311
	Slaughtering and Meat Packing	92,554,000	30,743,107
	Flour and Grist Mill Products	65,448,000	27,077,833
OREGON			
1860	Flour	1,178,050	396,400
	Lumber, sawed	690,008	430,400
	Gold mining	210,000	83,000
	Saddlery and Harness	118,711	36,900
	Woolen Goods	85,000	70,000
1870	Flour and Grist Mill Products	1,972,444	1,116,825
	Lumber, sawed	1,014,211	913,262
	Woolen Goods	492,857	380,500
	Carpentering and Building	417,152	53,395
	Blacksmithing	286,176	90,063
1880	Flour and Grist Mill Products	3,475,531	1,286,200
	Lumber, sawed	2,030,463	1,577,875
	Woolen Goods	549,030	566,800
	Saddlery and Harness	385,350	190,050
	Foundry and Machine Shop Products	352,200	260,500

TABLE 4.4
(continued)

	Industry	Aggregate Value of Products	Aggregate Value of Capital
OREGON			
1890	Lumber and Timber	$ 6,530,757	$ 8,103,000
	Flour and Grist Mill Products	4,184,473	2,247,389
	RR Cars: Repairs and Construction	1,750,926	2,815,997
	Fish Canning and Preserving	1,643,324	1,365,800
	Slaughtering	1,570,935	439,600
1900	Lumber and Timber	10,352,167	8,167,433
	Flour and Grist Mill Products	6,364,023	3,172,997
	Fish Canning and Preserving	1,788,809	2,558,642
	Slaughtering	1,638,480	760,448
	Printing and Publishing	1,078,337	1,312,263
1909	Lumber and Timber Products	30,200,000	35,030,556
	Flour and Grist Mill Products	8,891,000	5,669,890
	Slaughtering and Meat Packing	5,880,000	2,481,137
	Printing and Publishing	5,041,000	3,457,464
	Butter, Cheese and Cond. Milk	4,920,000	1,718,068

TABLE 4.4
(continued)

	Industry	Aggregate Value of Products	Aggregate Value of Capital
OREGON			
1919	Lumber and Timber Products	$ 85,348,000	$ 83,482,424
	Flour and Grist Mill Products	42,550,000	23,099,592
	Foundry and Machine Shop Products	21,136,00	7,388,394
	Slaughtering and Meat Packing	15,868,000	5,255,407
	Shipbuilding, wood	13,778,000	9,667,360
WASHINGTON			
1860	Lumber, sawed	1,172,520	1,166,000
	Flour and Meal	75,800	40,000
	Fisheries, oyster	44,597	18,000
	Coal, bituminous	32,244	25,000
	Shingles	21,840	2,000
1870	Lumber, sawed	1,307,585	1,285,202
	Lumber, planed	616,100	110,900
	Flour and Grist Mill Products	321,103	188,300
	Carpentering and Building	87,973	12,285
	Blacksmithing	85,761	30,800

TABLE 4.4
(continued)

	Industry	Aggregate Value of Products	Aggregate Value of Capital
WASHINGTON			
1880	Lumber, sawed	$ 1,734,742	$ 2,456,450
	Shipbuilding	184,500	33,000
	Blacksmithing	160,175	55,225
	Saddlery and Harness	156,880	72,500
	Flour and Grist Mill Products	114,086	42,300
1890	Lumber and Timber Products	17,450,301	21,400,307
	Flour and Grist Mill Products	2,460,809	1,140,630
	Lumber, Planing Mill Products	2,030,279	899,765
	Printing and Publishing	1,678,541	1,197,108
	Foundry and Machine Shop Products	1,347,700	938,780
1900	Lumber and Timber	30,286,280	26,041,089
	Flour and Grist Mill Products	6,875,672	2,693,282
	Fish Canning and Preserving	4,831,038	2,222,726
	Foundry and Machine Shop Products	2,257,643	1,629,377
	Printing and Publishing	1,855,730	1,159,166

TABLE 4.4
(continued)

	Industry	Aggregate Value of Products	Aggregate Value of Capital
WASHINGTON			
1909	Lumber and Timber Products	$89,155,000	$ 97,224,264
	Flour and Grist Mill Products	17,853,000	11,077,186
	Slaughtering and Meat Packing	15,654,000	5,103,334
	Fruit and Vegetable, Can and Preserve	9,595,000	7,355,195
	Printing and Publishing	9,286,000	5,867,064
1919	Lumber and Timber Products	220,512,000	159,411,073
	Shipbuilding, steel	140,980,000	103,019,540
	Flour and Grist Mill Products	81,141,000	39,058,570
	Slaughtering and Meat Packing	34,389,000	12,759,109
	Shipbuilding, wood	25,539,000	17,703,162

SOURCES FOR TABLE 4.4

1860: 1860 United States Census, *Manufactures of the United States.* California: 35–36; Oregon: 492; Washington: 673.

1870: 1870 United States Census, *Statistics of the Wealth and Industry of the United States.* California: 497–498; Oregon: 561; Washington: 580. ("Quartz, milled" is assumed to represent mined gold)

1880: 1880 United States Census, volume 2: *Manufactures.* California: 92–94; Oregon: 165–166; Washington: 186–187.

1890: 1900 United States Census, volume 8: *Manufactures*, part 2. California: 35; Oregon: 733; Washington: 924–925.

1900: same source as 1890 data.

1909: 1910 United States Census, *Reports by States*, Supplement. California: volume 1, 677 and 706–709; Oregon: volume 7, 652 and 666–667; Washington: volume 9, 654 and 672–673.

1919: 1920 United States Census, volume 9: *Manufactures.* California: 84 and 112–120; Oregon: 1237 and 1252–1255; Washington: 1554 and 1572–1577.

Mining

Gold mining, which was the spark to the major population and production increase on the Pacific Coast, did not at first require much in the way of capital. Placer mining--taking gold from riverbeds--was the dominant form of mining for the first year or two of the gold rush. This method required little more than a simple pan or some type of strainer to separate gold from river gravel. However, with the depletion of easily-found river gold, prospectors had to turn to quartz mining in which gold had to be extracted from veins in solid rock. Ira Cross calls this transition the start of the industrial revolution in the region, since the technique was very capital-intensive.[48] Tools were required to remove the rock, and stamp mills were needed to pulverize the rock into fine powder from which the gold could be precipitated with the use of mercury. In fact, the capital inputs were so large that most individual miners were replaced by corporations or joint stock companies. Hydraulic mining, which first appeared in 1853, (and which left irreparable scars on California hillsides) also required investment in hoses and flumes to channel water to the gold-bearing dirt. The 1860 U.S. Census lists over seven thousand gold mining operations, with a total capital stock of more than eleven million dollars.

Both the huge mining industry in California and western Nevada, and the continuing mining activity in the states of the Pacific Northwest, kept up the demand for equipment to run the mines and the mills. San Francisco was the leading producer of such equipment, both because funds were available there to finance manufactories, and because the expertise required to design equipment appropriate to Western mines resided in the city. Consequently, both the equipment and the funds to purchase the equipment were to be found in San Francisco, and most Sierra Nevada mines, and a good part of the mines of the Pacific Northwest were owned by San Franciscans.[49]

Wheat and Flour

Wheat, which dominated the agricultural sector in both California and the Pacific Northwest through the 1890s, had differing capital requirements in the different states. Wheat agriculture in

California was more highly mechanized than in the Midwest. The capital requirements resulted from the conjunction of very large land holdings and relatively scarce labor. During the 1850s when owners of Mexican land grants were battling to prove their claims, the lengthy nature of the process often resulted in the forfeiture of land claims to moneylenders. This, along with the sale of large tracts of railroad land to single buyers in California resulted in highly concentrated land ownership.[50] For example, Hugh J. Glenn started buying land on credit in the Sacramento Valley in 1867; he eventually acquired a total of 55,000 acres in the area, which he planted in wheat.[51] Huge steam-driven combine harvesters were particularly useful on the flat, dry land of California's Central Valley.

The Pacific Northwest, on other hand, was slower to adopt such farm machinery. This is partly the consequence of the more hilly terrain in the wheat-growing regions of eastern Oregon and Washington, and of the late expansion of the industry into the Northwest. But wheat ranching rapidly mechanized after 1900, especially in the larger farms of Oregon.[52] The first such machinery for Oregon wheat farms came from California.[53]

While a large part of the wheat grown in the Pacific Coast region was exported as grain to Britain (the dryness of the grain made it especially suited to shipment by sea), substantial amounts of capital were invested in flour and grist mills in the late nineteenth century. Mills tended to cluster in cities such as San Francisco and Portland where large amounts of funds were available. California's mills produced output whose value exceeded all other manufacturing concerns in 1870 and 1880; more than two million dollars were invested in these mills in 1870. These mills were even more important in the Oregon economy; their products were in the top one or two manufacturing concerns, by value, from 1860 to 1919. As early as 1890, the mills were using more than eight million dollars of capital. The flour and grist mills of Washington contained at least eleven million dollars of capital, but consistently lagged behind the lumber industry in capital and product value.

Food Processing

The canning and preserving industries processed the fruits and vegetables of the region, as well as the abundant supply of fish harvested from the waters of the Pacific Ocean. The processing of fresh fruits and vegetables increased rapidly after 1900 in California; in that year, the state was producing 25 per cent of the nation's canned fruits and vegetables,[54] and was using a capital stock of more than four million dollars. By 1919, this industry accounted for almost 64 million dollars in capital. The industry was also important in Washington, where it ranked fourth in value of production among the state's industries in 1910. Such processing was a necessary procedure prior to the advent of fast and efficient refrigerated transportation; it allowed the diversified agricultural base of the region to enjoy a nationwide market. The canning and preserving of fish was an important industry for both Oregon and Washington between 1890 and 1910; Californians were major entrepreneurs in the canneries of the Pacific Northwest and Alaska.[55]

The other large agricultural processing venture on the Coast was the sugar refining industry in California. The first refinery was built on San Francisco Bay in 1860 to process cane from the Hawaiian Islands. The beet sugar industry was founded in Alameda County in 1870, although the industry did not establish itself solidly until the 1890s.[56] A large amount of capital was required to process cane and beet sugar, whose value exceeded all other manufacturing industries in California in the 1890s and 1900s. As early as 1890, three sugar processors accounted for more than 5.5 million dollars in capital.

Lumber, Timber, and Paper

The lumber and timber industries, exploiting the abundant forest resources of the Pacific Northwest, arose from the numerous small sawmills set up near the stumpage (the stands of trees) to provide for the needs of housing and mine construction during the gold rush. The cargo mill trade to Hawaii, the expanding mining industry, and the booming population of the entire Pacific Coast region gave tremendous impetus to the lumber industry. The construction of the railways in the 1870s and 1880s both absorbed much of the output of the mills and opened up the eastern market for Pacific Coast region lumber. The lumber industry required not only investment in the sawmills themselves, but also construction of logging railroads to transport timber from stands to mills.[57] It was common for the amount of capital invested in the industry to exceed the value of its yearly production in all the states. In fact, the lumber and timber products industry in each of the states accounted for more of the states' capital stock than any other single industry. San Francisco capitalists were major financiers of these mills, as in the case of Pope and Talbot, which was established as an export agency in San Francisco in the 1850s. The agency decided that greater profits were to be had through backward integration, so it set up a sawmill on Puget Sound in 1853 to produce for the company's export trade.[58]

Paper and pulp mills also used the abundant timber stands of the Pacific Northwest. While the industry did not grow to export size until the 1920s, it did produce paper for regional use before that date. However, it has been suggested that the capital requirements for paper and pulp mills were so high that the industry was discouraged, and timber was used in the profitable lumber industry instead.[59] The mills that did exist in the late nineteenth century, especially those mills located in Washington, were largely owned by San Francisco entrepreneurs. The familiar name of Zellerbach and the Crown Zellerbach company could be seen on mills in California, Oregon and Washington late in the century.[60]

The abundant natural resources available for papermaking proved useful. The highly educated, urban population of the Coast, and the availability of large amounts of savings held by a few families in California (particularly the Hearst and Scripps families) made the printing and publishing industries important on the Coast in the early twentieth century. The printing and publishing industry ranked in the top five in value of output between 1890 and 1909 in the Pacific Northwest states, and had almost six million dollars in capital in 1909.

Other Industries

Woolens were an important product in Oregon in the 1870s and 1880s, with the nationally-known Pendleton mills leading the industry. In the late 1880s, open range cattle grazing in the Pacific Northwest had given way to wheat farming and sheep ranching. As early as 1880, the states of the Pacific Northwest were producing approximately five percent of U.S. wool clip.[61] Wool's high ratio of value to bulk made profitable the production of wool for export to California mills. Some Oregon mills were joint-stock ventures financed locally,[62] since the capital requirements were not insurmountable. But in 1880, the entire industry only accounted for one-half million dollars in capital in Oregon.

Other major industries on the Coast which were later entrants into the top ranks of production value are petroleum and shipbuilding. The petroleum industry began in California with the formation of the Pacific Coast Oil Company in 1878. The founders were United States Senator Charles Felton, and Well Fargo official Lloyd Tevis, two "venture capitalists" from San Francisco. This company later became the basis for Standard Oil Company (of California), when Standard Oil purchased the Pacific Coast Oil Company in 1900. Petroleum refining produced more than two hundred million dollars of output, and required 84 million dollars in capital in 1919. Individual firm size was quite large, with average capital stock of two million dollars.

Shipbuilding was catapulted to prominence by the needs of World War I. By 1919, wood shipbuilding was in the top five industries, by value of product, in both Oregon and Washington. Washington also became a major producer of steel ships; the capital requirements in that industry were high, with an average firm investment of 11 million dollars in 1919.

CALIFORNIA INVESTMENT IN THE PACIFIC REGION

It is clear that some kind of financial network would need to be in place to facilitate the transfer of savings from the population into these investment projects. This is especially true in light of the recurring flow of savings from San Francisco residents into capital in the rest of the region. It also seems clear that the youth of the region, along with the high levels of per capita income, made available (especially in the most populous state of California) large amounts of savings which could be recycled at home. The residents of the region were not, for the most part, poor immigrants; the cost of the journey to the region precluded that. While income and savings figures are not available prior to 1880, we do have estimates for 1880 and 1920 produced by Richard Easterlin. Table 4.5 presents estimates of income, saving rates, and investment rates in the Pacific Coast states. What stands out is the conjunction of very high incomes and high saving to income and investment to income ratios in the area. Furthermore, a comparison of total saving and investment in each state

TABLE 4.5

INCOME, SAVING, AND INVESTMENT IN THE PACIFIC COAST STATES

1880—1920	Average Income ($ m)	Total Saving ($ m)	Total Investment ($ m)	Average S/Y (%)	Average I/Y (%)
California	1,880	14,104	10,400	18.8	13.8
Oregon	312	1,803	2,579	14.4	20.7
Washington	532	3,360	4,206	15.8	19.8
United States	39,008	219,229	220,081	14.0	14.1

NOTES: Data are from Richard Easterlin, "State Income Estimates," in *Population Redistribution and Economic Growth, United States, 1870–1950*, I, eds. Simon Kuznets and Dorothy Swaine Thomas (Philadelphia: American Philosophical Society, 1957), 729–733, 753.

Average income is found by simple arithmetic average of personal income in 1880 and in 1920. Total saving is derived by differencing the 1880 and 1920 figures for value of nonagricultural wealth owned by residents of a state; investment is derived by differencing the values for nonagricultural wealth located in a state.

Saving and investment rates [S/Y and I/Y] are estimated by calculating average yearly saving and investment (total saving and investment between 1880 and 1920, divided by 40) and expressing as a fraction of average yearly income.

leads one to the conclusion (as it did Lance Davis) that it is likely that California was an important source of the net capital imports into Oregon and Washington. Some mechanism would be needed to transfer those savings from California to the rest of the region.[63]

Here, again, we see a unique conjunction of events: a chronologically young state, California, is exporting capital in the same manner as older states such as New York and Massachusetts. This clearly results from California's phenomenal growth, and the establishment of a regional financial market born of wealth and isolation which facilitated the dispersion of California funds throughout the Pacific Coast region. This benefitted the wealth holders, who otherwise would have to place their funds in idle hoards, send their funds outside the region, or invest their funds themselves. It also benefitted the borrowers, who otherwise would have to save for self-finance, seek funds from outside the region, or ignore profitable investment opportunities.

While this situation of a new frontier region with extremely high income levels (and so very high levels of savings) was unique in the experience of the United States, the patterns of capital flows from San Francisco and California to the rest of the region generally followed the patterns of capital flows from any richer, more developed area to a newer, less developed area. That is, similar to the model of Harold Innis applied by Douglass North, much of the early investment by San Franciscans in the Pacific Coast region occurred in the production of export staple goods (such as wheat and lumber) and in the infrastructure required to transport and store those goods (such as railroads and warehouses).[64] The in-region financial metropolis of San Francisco acted in much the same capacity as far older financial centers such as New York City or London.

GROUPS IN EARLY FINANCIAL DEVELOPMENT

This concentration on the finance of export or traded goods and the infrastructure needed to market them is the consequence of the preeminence of commercial channels and merchandising profits in the development of a new region. As explained in previous chapters, the foundations of financial networks and financial flows in developing regions lie in the commercial channels and the profits of the merchants.[65] Consequently, the first flows of funds tend to be from merchants' wealth into the production of those goods whose trade yielded the merchant profits in the first instance. Furthermore, the first major networks of financial flows are based on personal relationships between merchants and merchant bankers. As Leff has pointed out (and as people like Naomi Lamoreaux have further investigated) such "groups" perform the principal functions of a capital market in a less developed region and "facilitate the flow of information and reduce the uncertainty that would otherwise raise the costs of investment throughout the economy."[66] The salient features of merchants within those groups are, as discussed in Chapter 3, that merchants have the first profit base in commercial economies, and that they have information on investment opportunities observed during their trading activities. They tend to either invest in inventories of goods, so stimulating the production of those goods, or they invest in the actual production of export goods or import-substituting goods.

Two groups[67] centered on San Francisco in the mid to late nineteenth century were, in particular, chief motivators of savings into investment projects throughout the Pacific Coast region. The relationships among these men were ultimately formalized into institutional financial linkages, but their ability to mobilize capital in the region had its foundation in personal trust. The groups were born in the mineral wealth and merchandising profits of the California gold rush and the Comstock silver boom of the mid-nineteenth centuries; the networks they established survived far into the twentieth century.

The two groups, known popularly as the "Big Four" and the "Silver Kings" each consisted of four men, with interlinkages through one man's bank--not a unique circumstance in so centralized a world as financial San Francisco in the mid-1800s. The Big Four was comprised of Charles Crocker, Leland Stanford, Collis Huntington, and Mark Hopkins. These men began their careers as merchants in Sacramento, supplying goods to gold miners. The profits to be made on such trade were tremendous, considering the extremely high demand and relatively inelastic supply conditions during the gold rush. Their merchandising profits from the gold rush period, and the expected profits from their Comstock Lode trade made these men clear targets for Theodore Judah, an engineer with a plan for a transcontinental railway. After having approached financiers in San Francisco with no success[68] Judah presented his plan in 1860 to the four Sacramento merchants, and he emphasized the profits to be found in construction of a line over whose route goods could be carried to the Comstock miners.

Judah's pitch was successful. The Central Pacific Railroad of California was incorporated on June 28, 1860; each of the Big Four subscribed 150 shares of stock at one hundred dollars per share, with ten percent paid in. The Pacific Railroad Act of 1862 assured that federal government support would be forthcoming for the railroad as it built eastward from Sacramento. One estimate is that the personal fortunes the men would ultimately gain from the railway totalled 200 million dollars.[69] These returns came largely in the form of profits from companies they owned and organized to build the railway (chiefly, the Contract and Finance Company, which was the counterpart to the Union Pacific Railway's Credit Mobilier), and from monopoly rates they charged over their lines. Eventually, the railways controlled by the Big Four spanned the Pacific Coast region, and were consolidated under the guise of the Southern Pacific Railroad.

On the outskirts of the Big Four was William Chapman Ralston. Ralston began his career as a shipping agent in Panama, but he eventually went on to become the director of San Francisco's Bank of California, the first institution to incorporate as a commercial bank under the California bank incorporation law of 1864.[70] As Julian Dana put it, "This bank, in its first breath of life, became the financial and commercial arbiter of the Pacific Coast. And Billy Ralston *was* the Bank of California."[71] Through this bank, Ralston financed a wide range of ventures, including the Central Pacific Railroad. Ralston gave Stanford and Hopkins an unsecured one-quarter million dollar loan for the line; over the years the bank's loans to the railroad totalled more than three million dollars.[72]

The great power of the Bank of California on the Coast, and its eventual downfall, came from the bank's foreclosure upon Comstock mine mortgages during the lode's decline in the 1860s. With heavy investment of new capital, deeper deposits of ore were tapped, and the resources of the Bank of California skyrocketed.[73] Ralston's attempt to gain control of the Ophir mine through stock purchases ultimately bankrupted the institution in 1875, forcing the bank to suspend payments. Ralston, it is speculated, committed suicide the day after he was relieved as director; the bank reopened with Darius O. Mills as president.[74]

The Bank of California's mines and mills were taken over by the "Silver Kings": John Mackay, James Fair, James Flood, and William O'Brien. O'Brien and Flood were San Francisco saloon keepers who turned barroom conversation with stockbrokers into profitable careers trading on the San Francisco Mining Exchange; Mackay and Fair were Comstock mine superintendents. These four men came together in the late 1860s and early 1870s to buy up ownership of the Comstock mines. In 1873, their Consolidated Virginia mine struck huge new silver deposits, and the group made fortunes through the minerals they owned and through less-than-honest dealings on the mining exchange.[75]

Together, these two kinship groups (and their link through William Chapman Ralston) came to own or control a vast array of firms engaged in the production of export goods, residentiary goods, services, and infrastructure on the Pacific Coast. The Big Four, of course, dominated the transportation network throughout California. Through the Southern Pacific Railroad, they obtained control of the Oregon and California Railway to Portland, and the contract for the western link in the transcontinental route across the southern United States. In 1869, the Big Four purchased the California Steam Navigation Company to gain control of traffic between San Francisco and interior towns of California;[76] in 1874 they created the Occidental and Oriental Steamship Line to compete for traffic along the Coast. But they certainly were not limited to interest in the transportation sector. The Crocker-Woolworth Bank, timber in the Pacific Northwest, real estate development in San Francisco and in Southern California, and Leland Stanford Junior University are examples of the wide range of the Big Four's investment projects.

Ralston, through his own wealth and use of the Bank of California's funds, also financed a number of ventures throughout the region. These included transportation projects such as the Central Pacific Railroad, Hunter's Point Drydocks in San Francisco, and the Portland-based Oregon Steam Navigation Company.[77] He also invested heavily in the industrial sector of San Francisco which produced import-substituting goods for the residents of the Pacific Coast region. Included in his portfolio were investments in the California Sugar Refinery, the Pacific Woolen Mills, the Kimball Manufacturing Company (which produced railroad rolling stock), West Coast Furniture, and the Palace Hotel.

The Silver Kings, too, placed their wealth in a wide variety of ventures. Profits were to be had in companies which furnished supplies and services to the Comstock mines in the 1870s, including timber, water power, and mills. In 1875, the four incorporated the Nevada Bank in San Francisco, which eventually consolidated with Wells Fargo in 1891. It is interesting to note that an attempt was made in 1887 to corner the Coast market in wheat; this attempt was financed through the Nevada Bank. The failure of the venture produced such losses for the bank that it had to be supported with loans from the Silver King's old nemesis--Ralston's Bank of California.

What stands out about these stories are the close interlinkages of the groups, the breadth of their investments in export production and infrastructure, and their universal drive to form banks. These were not wildcat banks either. In one form or another, the Bank of California, the Crocker-Woolworth Bank, and the Nevada Bank still exist today. Chapter 5 will explore in more detail the financial institutions which succeeded the informal kinship groups to transfer savings throughout the Pacific Coast region in the late nineteenth and early twentieth centuries.

NOTES

1. The text will refer to these areas as "states" for purposes of clarity; it is understood that no states officially existed prior to date of admission.
2. Tattersall calls Captain James Cook's 1778 exploration of the fur trade the "first commercial contact with the Pacific Northwest." James Tattersall, "The Economic Development of the Pacific Northwest to 1920" (Ph.D., diss., University of Washington, 1960), 33.
3. Dorothy Johansen and Charles Gates, *Empire of the Columbia* (New York: Harper and Brothers, 1957), 226.
4. Portland, Oregon was founded in 1845; Seattle, Washington in 1849.
5. Thomas Senior Berry calls gold a good with "infinitely elastic demand." Berry, *Early California*, 97.
6. Jane Jacobs, *Cities and the Wealth of Nations* (New York: Random House, 1984), 145.
7. Walton Bean, *California: An Interpretive History* (New York: McGraw-Hill, 1978), 88-89.
8. For an extended discussion, see Bean, *California: An Interpretive History*, 89-92.
9. Berry, *Early California*, 74-75. Bean, *California: An Interpretive History* (100), puts the 1852 figure at approximately $80 million.
10. John Caughey, *Gold is the Cornerstone* (Berkeley: University of California Press, 1948), 292.
11. Bean, *California: An Interpretive History*, 165.
12. Tattersall, "Economic Development of the Pacific Northwest," 54.
13. Tattersall, "Economic Development of the Pacific Northwest," 43.
14. Bean, *California: An Interpretive History* (100), estimates that there were 100,000 miners working in 1852.
15. In fact, those who were engaged in support activities for miners were usually the ones who derived the greatest profits from the mining industry, as will be shown later.
16. The city of Seattle began as a camp producing lumber for the mining trade. Caughey, *Gold is the Cornerstone*, 213-214.

17. James Gilbert, "Trade and Currency in Early Oregon," in *Columbia University Studies in History, Economics, and Public Law* 26 (1907), 76.
18. See Gilbert, "Trade and Currency," on the return flow of labor to Oregon.
19. Tattersall, "Economic Development of the Pacific Northwest," 58-59.
20. See Tattersall, "Economic Development of the Pacific Northwest."
21. Bean, *California: An Interpretive History*, 167.
22. Bean, *California: An Interpretive History*, 135.
23. Tattersall, "Economic Development of the Pacific Northwest," 43.
24. Johansen and Gates, *Empire of the Columbia*, 390.
25. Bean, *California: An Interpretive History*, 167-168.
26. Margery Saunders ["California Wheat, 1867-1910: Influences of Transportation on the Export Trade and the Location of Producing Areas" (M.A. thesis, University of California, 1960), 104] also attributes the decline of California's wheat trade to a reduction in freight rates which lowered the British price paid to producers.
27. See Carey McWilliams, [*California: The Great Exception* (New York: A.A. Wyn, 1949), 32, 216] for an interesting outlook on distance as tariff.
28. The vast stretches of agricultural land in the interior of Washington were difficult to tap, since no river flowed from these areas to the Sound. The exploitation of this land was postponed until the completion of rail lines in the 1880s.
29. The Northern Pacific Railroad had built a connection between Portland and Puget Sound by 1874.
30. This was also true of water transportation; few shiploads from the eastern seaboard went directly to the Pacific Northwest without transshipment through San Francisco. Arthur Throckmorton, "The Role of the Merchant on the Oregon Frontier: The Early Business Career of Henry W. Corbett, 1851-1869," *Journal of Economic History* 16 (December 1956), 545.

31. Actually, the Central Pacific Railroad had built east from Sacramento, whose water routes to San Francisco were well-established. The rail line to San Francisco Bay was completed in 1870.
32. James Hedges, *Henry Villard and the Railways of the Northwest* (New Haven: Yale University Press, 1930), 1.
33. See, Tattersall, "Economic Development of the Pacific Northwest," 249-250.
34. Also see Jacobs, *Cities and the Wealth of Nations*, Beverly Duncan and Stanley Lieberson, *Metropolis and Region in Transition* (Beverly Hills, California: Sage Publications, 1970); Robert Elgie, "The Development of San Francisco Manufacturing, 1848-1880: An Analysis of Regional Locational Factors and Urban Spatial Structure" (M.A. thesis, University of California, 1966); Roger Lotchin, *San Francisco, 1846-1856: From Hamlet to City* (New York: Oxford University Press, 1974); Gunther Barth, *Instant Cities: Urbanization and the Rise of San Francisco and Denver* (New York: Oxford University Press, 1975); Glenn Quiett, *They Built the West* (New York: Cooper Square, 1965); and James Vance, *Geography and Urban Evolution in the San Francisco Bay Area* (Berkeley: Institute of Government Studies, 1964).
35. Earl Pomeroy, *The Pacific Slope*, (New York: Alfred Knopf, 1965), 58.
36. See Myrdal, *Economic Theory and Under-Developed Regions*, and Allan Pred, *The Spatial Dynamics of U.S. Urban-Industrial Growth, 1800-1914* (Cambridge: MIT Press, 1966) for discussions of "initial advantage."
37. Tattersall, "Economic Development of the Pacific Northwest," 77; and 1880 US Census, volume 19, *Social Statistics of Cities*, part 2. Tattersall reports that the population of Seattle jumped to nearly 43,000 in 1890, after the transcontinental railroad had reached the city.
38. Bean, *California: An Interpretive History*, 94.
39. Hedges, *Henry Villard*, 343.
40. See Ira Cross [*Financing an Empire* (Chicago: S.J. Clarke, 1927), 365] regarding the inflow of Chicago merchants.

41. The Civil War had also acted as a stimulus to the Pacific region's own development by increasing the effective isolation of the area through increasing transportation costs.
42. McWilliams, *California: The Great Exception*, 32.
43. Duncan and Lieberson, *Metropolis and Region in Transition*, follow in the tradition of Gras, *An Introduction to Economic History*, outlining the stages of metropolitan development.
44. Vance, *Geography and Urban Evolution*, 18.
45. Elgie ["Development of San Francisco Manufacturing," 59], claims that since most of California's trade passed through San Francisco, the profits made in that trade tended to accumulate in San Francisco.
46. Code ["The Spatial Dynamics of Financial Intermediaries," 155] makes this same point, calling the assumption of financial services by outside centers "pirating."
47. Code, "Spatial Dynamics of Financial Intermediaries," 254.
48. Cross, *Financing an Empire*, 234.
49. See Tattersall ["Economic Development of the Pacific Northwest," 210-212] for a discussion of the sources of mine finance in the Pacific Northwest.
50. The Miller and Lux cattle ranch in the San Joaquin Valley encompassed a strip on either side of the Sacramento River, 100 miles long. The two men owned more than one million acres throughout the Pacific Coast region.
51. Bean, *California: An Interpretive History*, 227.
52. Tattersall, "Economic Development of the Pacific Northwest," 177.
53. Gordon Dodds, *Oregon: A Bicentennial History* (New York: Norton, 1977), 132.
54. Robert Cleland and Osgood Hardy, *March of Industry* (Los Angeles: Powell, 1929), 85.
55. See Dodds, *Oregon*, 79.
56. Bean, *California: An Interpretive History*, 51, 87-88.
57. See Thomas Cox, *Mills and Markets: A History of the Pacific Coast Lumber Industry to 1900* (Seattle: University of Washington Press, 1974), 125-126. He estimates the cost of one mile of logging railroad at $30,000 (261).
58. See Cox, *Pacific Coast Lumber Industry*, 61.

59. Tattersall, "Economic Development of the Pacific Northwest," 244.
60. See Reed Hunt, *Pulp, Paper and Pioneers: The Story of Crown Zellerbach Corporation* (New York: The Newcomen Society, 1961).
61. Tattersall, "Economic Development of the Pacific Northwest," 64.
62. See Alfred Lomax, *Pioneer Woolen Mills in Oregon* (Portland, Oregon: Binfords and Mort, 1941), 101.
63. Admittedly, these data are only indicative of the relationship between the states. Census figures used in construction of the estimates are not completely reliable; however, Richard Easterlin has expressed confidence in their ability to reflect capital flows.
64. Douglass North, "International Capital Flows and the Development of the American West," *Journal of Economic History* 16 (December 1956), 493-505.
65. See Porter and Livesay, *Merchants and Manufacturers*, among others.
66. Nathaniel Leff, "Capital Markets in the Less Developed Countries: The Group Principle" in Ronald McKinnon, ed. *Money and Finance in Economic Growth and Development* (New York: Marcel Dekker, 1976), 99.
67. "Groups" are defined by Leff [1976] as people linked by communal, tribal, ethnic, or personal relations of trust and mutual confidence.
68. These capitalists apparently did not recognize the profits available in construction of the railway or in the use of the lines to supply the rest of the Pacific Coast. No doubt the risk associated with the operation and the possibility that the railway would remove the tariff of distance from the east discouraged some financiers. Nash suggests that their unwillingness may also have resulted from the provision in the California Constitution which mandated unlimited liability of corporate directors. Gerald Nash, *State Government and Economic Development* (Berkeley: Institute of Government Studies, 1964), 56.
69. Bean, *California: An Interpretive History*, 175.

70. Prior to this, banks incorporated under the general incorporation law and operated under the guise of merchant houses or even manufacturers.
71. Julian Dana, *The Man Who Built San Francisco* (New York: Macmillan, 1936), 177.
72. See Cross, *Financing an Empire*, 284, and Dana, *The Man Who Built San Francisco*, 229.
73. Bean, *California: An Interpretive History*, 191.
74. See Kerry Ann Odell, "William Chapman Ralston and the Golden Beginnings of Finance on the Pacific Coast" (Paper presented to Bancroft Readers' Roundtable, June 1986) for further comments on the life and times of William Chapman Ralston.
75. Bean, *California: An Interpretive History*, 193.
76. Oscar Lewis, *The Big Four* (New York: Alfred Knopf, 1938), 363.
77. See Quiett, *They Built the West*, 344.

CHAPTER 5

San Francisco and Its Institutional Network

The history of the Pacific Coast region, as well as other regions such as the Northeast[1] have pointed out the key roles played in early development by personal savings and investment, especially by merchants, and the informal networks created among residents to mobilize savings. As time progresses, we see the broadening of investment opportunities into non-export industries (import-substituting, residentiary, footloose) and the dispersion of savings into the hands of labor and capitalists engaged in productive activity. The consequence of this broadened base of both investment and saving is the need for more formalized, less personal means of accumulating savings and mobilizing them to profitable opportunities.

INDIVIDUAL FINANCIAL INSTITUTIONS

> Social overhead capital. . . required great investment and led associations and individuals to establish financial institutions--banks, insurance companies, and stock exchanges--for the mobilization and accumulation of funds.[2]

What is interesting about the Pacific experience is that it was San Francisco, an internal center, which developed institutions to mobilize regional funds into regional projects. The list of institutions used to facilitate funds transfers was as varied in the Pacific region as it had been in the older regions of the East Coast. Some of the more important institutions, many of which have ties to the informal personal networks discussed previously, will be presented in this chapter.

Commercial Banks

As mentioned in Chapter 4, the formalization or institutionalization of financial connections first appeared in commercial banks. This was clearly the case with Ralston's Bank of California, and with the Nevada Bank of the Silver Kings. These two banks formed the basis for, or became part of, two important regional financial networks. One of these was the Bank of California banking group which reached into Oregon and Washington; the other was the Wells Fargo organization which had blanketed the West since the 1850s, and into which the Nevada Bank merged. Each of these institutional networks will be discussed in turn.

The Bank of California has already been introduced in the discussion of its founder, William Chapman Ralston. It was during Ralston's reign (1864-1875) that this bank expanded its market territory. As Hunter writes, "With the entire western third of the Nation in which to operate, the bank promptly made its influence felt in many fields. Under the direction of William C. Ralston, whose faith in the future of the region was unbounded, numerous enterprises designed to speed its development received encouragement and support."[3] Ralston, in fact, had broken off ties with his New York shipping partners in the 1850s precisely because those men felt Ralston was interested in investing too much of the firm's capital in the Coast region.[4]

Much of the Bank's net worth which facilitated a regional investment strategy was the result of a well-timed and well-executed branching effort by the institution. Ralston had placed an agent, William Sharon, in Virginia City, Nevada. Because of timely information and expertise in mining, Sharon was able to tempt mine owners into heavy borrowing at low interest rates. After a number of foreclosures upon owners unable to meet debt payments when the first Comstock boom ended in the mid-1860s, the Bank acquired a major portion of the mines and mills in the area. These were consolidated into the Union Mill and Mining Company under Sharon's management.

With bank funds, new machinery was installed to seek deeper deposits of ore. Millions of dollars of output were eventually taken out of the Bank's mines, providing the basis for the institution's expanded activity in various investment projects. These investments were arranged primarily through William Ralston, either through investment advice he gave or through personal loans to him. Ralston borrowed three million dollars alone to buy the Spring Valley Water Company, an engineering project designed to carry water to San Francisco.

The interesting point about the later development of this bank (it exists still) is that it was the only bank in the nation which operated branches across state lines.[5] Sharon's agency in Virginia City was not a true branch bank; it existed mainly to channel loan business to the head office in San Francisco. In 1905, however, the Bank did acquire three full-service branches in the Pacific Northwest. A merger in that year with the foreign-chartered London and San Francisco Bank gave the Bank of California branches in Portland, Seattle, and Tacoma. The London and San Francisco Bank, established in 1865, had placed its first branch in Portland in 1882 to finance the movement of wheat from the Columbia basin to Europe. The merger in 1905 gave the Bank of California the head office in San Francisco as well as the branches in Oregon and Washington; the bank was allowed to keep the out-of-state branches.

In 1852, in response to the lure of business in California, Wells, Fargo and Company was founded as a joint stock association in New York City. The company was organized to convey all types of material--mail and freight--between New York and San Francisco, and to collect miners' bullion and gold dust for shipment to the East. The company rapidly spread outward from its headquarters in San Francisco into the Pacific Northwest, by creating a hub in Portland only seven months after the establishment of the main office, and by setting up an agency on Puget Sound in 1857. By 1880, there were nineteen offices in Washington and fifty in Oregon; Idaho and Nevada were also crisscrossed by Wells Fargo routes.[6]

What is important about such express companies, of which Wells Fargo was the most geographically far-reaching, is that banking was a natural adjunct of the business. The California Constitution of 1849 forbade the issue of bank notes and the incorporation of banks; all banks had to be privately owned.[7] Many institutions did banking business while ostensibly acting as manufacturing firms incorporated under the general incorporation laws of 1853. The express companies became de facto banking house, holding miners' gold and issuing certificates of deposit. The companies also bought and sold gold dust and bullion, and bills of exchange--typical functions of primitive banks set up to facilitate trade. One express company official wrote that "The miners had no opportunity for taking care of their dust, and we were obliged to have safes at our different offices, and our express business soon merged into a banking business."[8] The Oregon Constitution of 1857 included California's prohibition of bank incorporation and bank note issue, but Wells Fargo Company survived in the Pacific Northwest as it had in California, by acting as a private institution issuing certificates of deposit, not bank notes.

In 1866, Wells Fargo consolidated with Ben Holladay's Overland Mail, the Pioneer Stage Company, American Express, and the US Express Company. The resulting company had a capital stock of ten million dollars and controlled almost all overland express and mail business west of the Mississippi River.[9] Wells Fargo's banking business was separated from its express business in 1876.[10] The San Francisco headquarters obtained permanent footholds in Salt Lake City in 1865 with the purchase of Holladay's bank, and in Portland when Wells Fargo and Company secured the controlling interest in the Commercial National Bank in that city in 1893.[11]

A turning point for the Wells Fargo Bank occurred in 1890 when Isaias Hellman, president of the Farmers and Merchants Bank of Los Angeles, was called to San Francisco by the directors of the Nevada National Bank. Ira Cross writes that the directors requested that Hellman take active management of the bank;[12] it is more likely that Hellman himself was actively looking for entrance into the San Francisco market. In any case, "he was impressed with the opportunities afforded by the bustling financial center of the Pacific Coast, and in company with certain well known San Francisco capitalists purchased the bank and assumed control."[13] In 1905, Hellman's Nevada National Bank merged with the Wells Fargo Bank, with the intention of strengthening the Nevada Bank. Hellman, however, limited the possible scope of the business by selling all the Nevada National's branches prior to the merger. He also sold Wells Fargo's remaining branches in Portland and Salt Lake City, reportedly because he "did not care for branches."[14]

Unfortunately, the loan portfolios of the Wells Fargo Bank are unknown, possibly because the bank did not grant loans in the manner typical today, but instead allowed customers overdraft privileges.[15]

Company historians have found that loans were made to infrastructural concerns which facilitated Wells Fargo's express business. These included the Overland Mail Company, the Central Pacific Railroad, and the Southern Pacific Railroad.[16] Other investments of the bank included vineyards, wheat ranches, lumber, and mining companies in Nevada.[17]

Perhaps more important than individual loans was Wells Fargo's influence in opening the Pacific Coast region to commercial production. The assaying of gold, the sale of bills of exchange, and the transfer of funds to San Francisco and New York all facilitated the introduction of media of exchange and commercial transactions in the region. Furthermore, the vast network of agencies (there were over one thousand in 1883, including twenty-eight principal agencies, attached to San Francisco[18]) was an effective institutional information network. Agencies were created early in small mining towns, where it is said that "a billiard saloon, a restaurant, and a Wells & Fargo office are the first three elements. . . ."[19] These outlying agencies and principal offices in cities from Denver to Seattle, and Tucson to Honolulu, all fed information and specie into the main office in San Francisco. Such information, and the profits of the company (which totalled almost $200,000 in 1874 alone[20]) made Wells Fargo a powerful influence on the financial environment of the time, and re-emphasized the importance of San Francisco in accumulating and directing funds flows throughout the region.

Life Insurance Companies

The familiar names of Stanford, Huntington, and Ralston appear again when we consider the institutional form which has had greater impact in the long-term credit market than commercial banks. This is the life insurance company, which today rivals the banking sector in total assets. The development of incorporated insurance companies in California was hindered in the 1850s by the incorporation law which made directors and stockholders jointly and personally liable for all debts, but the companies' growth increased after 1861.[21] Life insurance companies, in particular, were large buyers of mortgages and corporate bonds (railroad, utilities) which had long maturities appropriate for investment of the companies' reserves. An important social overhead project to which capital needed to be mobilized was the transcontinental railroad. Leland Stanford and Collis Huntington founded the Pacific Mutual Life Insurance Company in 1867 for the purpose of accumulating funds with which to finance their railroad;[22] William Ralston was a director of the insurance company. A more altruistic motive for the establishment of the company was the desire to stem the outflow of insurance premiums to the East--premiums that were not, apparently, re-invested in the West.

A report on the insurance industry in the 1890 US Census shows a number of companies based in the Middle Atlantic region that listed the Pacific Coast region as part of their territory. The agents retained by such companies in Western cities (particularly in San Francisco) facilitated the outflow of premiums to the East.[23] Pritchett finds that the eastern insurance companies probably did not re-invest in the regions from which the premiums flowed. The Middle Atlantic region consistently provided a smaller percentage of premium income than was invested in those states by insurance companies in the late nineteenth century; the opposite was true for the South and the Pacific Coast regions.[24] The establishment of local companies to receive and re-invest premiums in the Pacific region was consequently a valid motive for incorporation.

The Pacific Mutual Life Insurance Company takes on added importance when one realizes that it was the only level premium life insurance company headquartered on the Pacific Coast as of 1890. Many of the eastern life insurance companies did business in California, but not in the less populous states of Oregon and Washington.[25] This opened up an opportunity for the entrance of California-based companies whose proximity to these states allowed greater information and monitoring capacity. By 1869, agencies of the Pacific Mutual had been established in Nevada (to cover Nevada, Idaho, and the Dakotas) and in Portland (to cover Oregon and "the Upper Coast").[26] Principal agencies were established in San Francisco in 1876, Los Angeles in 1877, and Arizona in 1879. The company's head office was transferred from Sacramento to San Francisco in 1881 because the latter city had "outdistanced the capital in growth and development and had become the metropolis of the Pacific Coast. The Company, located a hundred miles inland and quite to one side from the lines of development the state had taken, was finding it more and more difficult to secure an adequate amount of new business."[27]

It is not clear to what extent funds of policyholders in the region were recycled throughout the area. As in much research on financial flows during this period, the "two-headed monster" (C.I.D. Moore's term for the 1906 San Francisco earthquake and fire) destroyed many company records. Certainly, the Pacific Mutual might have been subject to the complaint that premiums were not re-invested at home. From Moore's work, we do know that funds were invested in Central Valley real estate and the Los Angeles Pacific Electric Railway.[28] The bulk of the company's assets was invested in real estate, contradicting the claim that it had been established only to channel funds into the Central Pacific Railroad. In 1886, of $1,150,554 in financial assets, $1,034,382 were invested in mortgage loans; almost thirty percent of these loans were on property located in Oregon and Washington.[29] This suggests an adequate re-investment flow, considering the smaller policyholder base in those states versus California. If anything, the claim may be made that premiums from the Pacific Northwest were drained into the financial center of San Francisco, where they were then re-invested in California real estate.

In 1905, the Conservative Life Insurance Company of Los Angeles, which owned approximately one-quarter of Pacific Mutual's stock, offered to buy out the stockholders of Pacific Mutual and merge the two companies. The offer was accepted, and the head office of the company was transferred to Los Angeles after the 1906 earthquake and fire.[30] Moore writes that this move "injected new life into the organization."[31] The late nineteenth century take-off of Los Angeles and the destruction of much of San Francisco in 1906 heralded the rise of the city in Southern California as a financial rival of San Francisco. While Los Angeles would not necessarily provide competition in the Pacific Northwest area, it would compete for San Francisco's business in Southern California and the Southwest. From a period in which Los Angeles was compelled to seek loans from "some banking house or moneylender in the distant financial center of 'the City,' San Francisco,"[32] new wealth from agriculture and petroleum provided a challenge to the old hierarchy in the first decade of the twentieth century.

Stock Exchanges

The other major financial institution involved in the long-term side of the market was the stock exchange. Both individuals and institutions benefitted (or should have) from the liquidity and information offered by these exchanges. As seems to be so often the case in the financial development of San Francisco and the Pacific Coast, the region gained a stock exchange very early in its history. San Francisco had, in the 1850s, many brokers dealing in steamboat, wharf, telegraph, water, "mining ditch", warehouse, and "other public service and industrial corporations."[33] But the prices of these stocks were not uniform across brokers, and volatility resulted from the lack of liquidity which an organized exchange could have provided.

No board of exchange was organized in the Pacific Coast region until the early 1860s when quartz mining became prevalent. As mentioned earlier, quartz mining required large investment in mining, milling, and refining equipment. The consequence was the formation of corporations which could tap wider pools of savings to finance the ventures. On the heels of such corporations came stock exchanges to trade in the ownership shares. The formation of such exchanges occur when stock is held in small amounts by numerous owners. If only large, institutional investors held stock, trades could be made on a negotiated basis between the few buyers and the few sellers.[34] The broad savings base in San Francisco made stock exchanges essential.

San Francisco was the natural site for the establishment of an exchange since

> under the conditions of communication that existed in the 1860's, and because of the highly specialized nature of mining stock exchanges, it was practicable to handle shares only fairly near the mining area. In San Francisco it was possible to judge with at least crude measures the profitability of individual mines; this would have been too risky in New York or Boston.[35]

Consequently, the San Francisco Stock and Exchange Board was organized in 1862; at its high point in 1875, seats sold for over $25,000. San Francisco traders employed agents near the mines to relay information of strikes; these were often transmitted in code to foil inquisitive telegraph operators along the route.[36] Potential investors outside the region could place orders on the stock exchange in San Francisco using the institutionalized information network embodied there. Orders from New York and Europe were placed on the exchange as early as the 1870s;[37] orders placed with William Ralston are found in his personal papers.

The exchange was primarily one of local issues, purchased with local funds. Pacific Coast region securities markets developed independently in response to savings surpluses of the region, and not in response to the growth of security trading in the rest of the nation.[38] The San Francisco-based exchanges were not branches of the New York Stock Exchange designed to channel regional savings to eastern corporations, but were true regional exchanges. Of course, the accumulation of small savers' funds to finance large corporate projects was not always looked upon with favor. In 1882, Robert Louis Stevenson called the stock exchange "the heart of San Francisco: a great pump we might call it, continually pumping up the savings of the lower quarters into the pockets of the millionaires upon the hill."[39]

Unlike other short-lived mining exchanges in the West, the San Francisco exchange did not die out when the mining booms were over. The phenomenal growth of the Pacific Coast region, and of California in particular, fueled the trade of corporate stocks and bonds. In 1904, the San Francisco Stock and Exchange Board absorbed the Pacific Stock Exchange (established 1875). By 1907, the list of companies whose stocks and bonds traded on the exchange included sixteen gas and electric companies, thirty-seven transportation companies, eight banks, eight water companies, oil companies, sugar refineries, and wine, borax, and fish packing concerns.[40] As with the migration of the Pacific Mutual Life Insurance Company, however, the stock exchanges in San Francisco eventually moved their headquarters to Southern California, where the larger part of the state's population and wealth were centered by the 1920s.

CORRESPONDENT BANK NETWORKS

In addition to the power of individual institutions to transfer funds through their own agencies or branches, formal affiliations of institutions can also efficiently mobilize savings across regions. Correspondent banking relationships have been considered extremely important in determining the flows of information and funds through the financial system in the nineteenth and twentieth centuries. John James, in particular, cites the correspondent system as a prime actor in the integration of capital markets in the United States.[41] A correspondent may hold the deposits of another bank's customers in its own bank, and it may notify other banks of large loans in which they might participate. Thus, the correspondent system can mobilize capital through the transfer of deposit location and through loan participations; correspondents are also efficient sources of information on economic conditions in other areas.

Although there are potential benefits from correspondent relationships, there are also potential costs. Richard Sylla has pointed out that correspondent relationships may actually drain funds out of less developed regions into the financial centers of the East,[42] thus creating an "uphill" flow of funds in the nation. The spatial analysis presented here would argue that this drain could result from poor regional networks which do not provide efficient channels through which local banks could recycle local funds, or through which outside banks might invest funds deposited with them. There occurs a type of "capital flight" similar to that seen in less developed countries today, as funds are placed with developed institutions which exist only outside the region or country. If correspondent networks are thick within the region, however, they can act to efficiently mobilize local funds at home. Ties to an in-region financial center with oversight power in the area (a clearinghouse for information on regional investment opportunities) can reduce the cost of investing regional funds at home. This financial center can take advantage of agglomeration economies, and re-direct local savings to the best use.

Rand McNally's *Banker's Directory* has published principal correspondent bank selections for each bank in the United States since 1876.[43] These data can be indexed both by the location of the bank and by the location of the correspondent chosen. Previous research, particularly by Michael Conzen, an economic geographer, has employed the data to analyze the changing urban hierarchy in the United States. Instead of focusing on the information about financial flows inherent in these networks, such research has used correspondent links as useful reflections of the status of cities as urban centers.[44] In the present study of regional financial markets, the extent of links between banks in different cities or states can provide independent estimates of financial networks which promote funds flows. Furthermore, changes in the number and direction of correspondent ties are an indication of changing financial market sizes and orientations.

Tables 5.1 and 5.2 present data on the major city correspondent chosen by Pacific Coast region banks. Some caution should be attached to the figures for New York City and Chicago. As central reserve cities under the National Bank Act, all reserve city banks were compelled to hold balances in one of these cities. Consequently, the selection of a New York City or a Chicago correspondent was not primarily motivated by financial or commercial interdependence with those cities. Forty-five to sixty percent of Pacific Coast bank balances held in New York City were legal reserves;[45] thus the western banks were not sending balances primarily for investment purposes or for loan participation. Approximately 25 percent of Coast balances in Chicago were legal reserves, suggesting that Chicago, not New York City, was the preferred depository for excess reserves or for funds for commercial clearings. Thus, it appears that the Pacific Coast region was more closely linked to Chicago than to New York City.

Table 5.1 indicates the importance of San Francisco as a correspondent for banks in the Pacific Coast region, especially in the earlier years when eighty percent of the Coast's banks had a correspondent in that city.[46] Also evident in Table 5.1 is the developing hierarchy of financial centers in the Pacific Coast region. As time progresses, the proportion of banks in outlying areas that choose closer in-state correspondents over San Francisco increases from approximately ten percent to more than ninety percent. However, Table 5.2 shows that the developing centers such as Portland and Seattle retain strong ties to San Francisco. In 1913, 83 percent of Portland banks and 72 percent of Washington city banks reported having a San Francisco correspondent.[47] Thus, while San Francisco's supremacy as a financial center was challenged at the beginning of the twentieth century, the city maintained significant influence over banking relationships in the region as the financial hierarchy deepened in the early twentieth century.

THE FEDERAL RESERVE SYSTEM

The official regionalization of financial affairs came with the establishment of the Federal Reserve System and the division of the United States into twelve Federal Reserve Districts in 1913. The development of this system is important to this research in two

TABLE 5.1

STATES' CORRESPONDENT CITY CHOICES

State	Date	#	% banks choosing NYC	% banks choosing CHI	% banks choosing SFO	% banks choosing in-state
CA	1883	116	83	9	84	0
	1893	253	90	13	82	4
	1903	314	104	47	95	22
	1913	766	80	34	90	33
OR	1883	23	78	4	87	9
	1893	97	94	18	48	37
	1903	97	99	47	69	81
	1913	253	75	41	38	93
WA	1883	18	56	0	89	11
	1893	157	94	22	25	20
	1903	136	90	38	38	78
	1913	371	82	36	16	95

NOTES: Data from Rand McNally Co., *The Banker's Directory of the United States and Canada* (Chicago, annual), volumes for years 1883, 1893, 1903, 1913.

= total of all national, state, and private banks in state reporting correspondent choices

" in-state" includes Los Angeles for California banks, Portland for Oregon banks, and Seattle, Spokane, and Tacoma for Washington banks

Percentages may exceed 100 because larger banks tended to choose more than one correspondent in the financial centers.

TABLE 5.2

CITIES' CORRESPONDENT CITY CHOICES

City	Date	#	% banks choosing NYC	% banks choosing CHI	% banks choosing SFO
San Francisco	1883	19	79	53	---
	1893	21	105	57	---
	1903	30	153	83	---
	1913	41	132	66	---
Los Angeles	1883	3	100	0	133
	1893	15	93	33	60
	1903	20	125	95	110
	1913	25	124	112	116
Portland	1883	8	75	13	88
	1893	19	100	47	47
	1903	14	121	71	78
	1913	23	117	83	83
WA cities	1883	5	80	0	100
	1893	44	86	36	23
	1903	28	104	78	54
	1913	54	115	76	72

NOTES: Data from Rand McNally's *Banker's Directory*, 1883, 1893, 1903, and 1913.

= total of all national, state, and private banks in city reporting correspondent choices

WA cities include Seattle, Spokane, and Tacoma

Percentages may exceed 100 because larger banks tended to choose more than one correspondent in the financial centers.

respects. It reiterates the supremacy of San Francisco as the financial center of the Pacific Coast region, if not the entire western United States. On the other hand, the controversy which arose over placing most of the western part of the country under the jurisdiction of the Federal Reserve Bank of San Francisco suggests again that the city's leadership in financial affairs was not unchallenged in the early twentieth century.

The Federal Reserve System was intended to reform the banking system of the United States and to provide for a more elastic currency; this issue has been well-documented. The aspect of the System key in this research is the division of the country into districts, each with a Federal Reserve Bank. The districting provision was a compromise between factions favoring a single central bank (similar to the Bank of England) and those opposing any centralized financial authority at all. Each Federal Reserve Bank was designed to be autonomous within its own district: forming policy, regulating members, and holding member bank reserves. To disturb traditional financial flows as little as possible, districts and their Reserve Banks were created to approximate commercial and financial patterns extant within the United States.

In hearings before the Senate, Dr. John Johnston, president of the National Reserve Bank of Kansas City, proposed that,

> in addition to these three central reserve cities [New York City, Chicago, and St. Louis], which good gumption would immediately be impressed with the fact that they should be each a Federal reserve city, there should be at least two more, one in San Francisco, and one in New Orleans.[48]

Dr. Johnston's case was not completely convincing. Upon polling banks within the states intended to comprise the New Orleans and the San Francisco Federal Reserve Districts, the hegemony of the two cities was challenged. New Orleans apparently held little sway over her own territory. Of more than four thousand first-, second-, and third-place votes cast for New Orleans, only 222 were from banks in the city's own territory.[49] This reflects New Orleans' greater importance as an interregional and international shipment center than as a regional financial center. New Orleans was bypassed, and Atlanta, whose position on railroad routes made her a more important regional center, was chosen as the Federal Reserve city for the Deep South.

The response to the proposal that San Francisco serve as the Federal Reserve city for the Coast states, Idaho, Nevada, Utah, and most of Arizona, was mixed. It is not clear how much of the opposition was based on lack of financial ties to the city, and how much was based on parochialism or even revenge against a too-dominant financial center. Clearly, San Francisco was still the largest center on the Pacific Coast; as of January 1914, national banks in San Francisco made over 100 million dollars in loans and discounts, while Los Angeles banks made less than one-half that amount, and national banks in Seattle and Portland made less than one-quarter.[50] Still, the rise of financial centers outside San Francisco, particularly in the Pacific Northwest, created pockets of opposition to San Francisco's appointment as Federal Reserve city. Table 5.3 displays the first-place votes cast for reserve cities by banks in the three most populous states in the Pacific Coast region. While San Francisco's dominance in California is clear, her strength in the Pacific Northwest is less certain.

Public hearings regarding Federal Reserve districting were held in seventeen cities nationwide in January 1914. Although "it was always unanimously agreed that the institutions at New York, Chicago and San Francisco were fundamentally essential and were to be regarded as basic in any scheme which was devised,"[51] the territory which was to be made tributary to San Francisco was very much under debate, as the votes listed in Table 5.3 indicate. Willis calls the Pacific Coast area "in many respects more nearly a single geographical area than the regions which border it to the east."[52] However, government officials held hearings in Portland and Seattle on the chance that this large western area would be split into a northern and a southern Federal Reserve district. Speakers at the Portland session were mild in their objections to a San Francisco district bank; they preferred to highlight Portland's importance within the Pacific Northwest, rather than her strength relative to San Francisco. Testimony revealed the fact that a majority of Portland banks did carry substantial balances with San Francisco banks "which were the natural result of their dealings with the southern part of the coast."[53]

In the Seattle hearings, however, the local "pride and prejudice" were vehemently presented, with representatives of Seattle claiming that they had more important business with Minneapolis and Chicago than with San Francisco and Los Angeles.[54] A closer reading

TABLE 5.3

FIRST–PLACE VOTES FOR
FEDERAL RESERVE BANK LOCATION

Proposed Bank	Banks in California	Banks in Oregon	Banks in Washington
San Francisco	208	16	8
Los Angeles	24		
Fresno		1	
Portland		56	9
Seattle			40
Spokane		1	16
New York City	2		

NOTES: Data from U.S. Congress, Senate, Federal Bank Organization Committee, *Letter to the Federal Reserve Board Relative to the Location of the Federal Reserve Banks* (63rd Cong., 2nd sess., 1914: S.Doc 485), 351–355.

Only national banks in each state voted.

of the testimony before these committees makes the objections of Washingtonians sound more like anti-monopoly sentiments than anti-efficiency arguments. One speaker from the Seattle Chamber of Commerce proclaimed,

> Nature has created and the lines of commerce support these two world outlets [San Francisco Bay and Puget Sound] on our western coast. It would seem proper that the regional bank divisions created by your committee should relate themselves normally with this great natural division, rather than to create an abnormally related district, tending to make one overshadowing financial center on the Pacific such as is New York on the Atlantic Coast.[55]

The weakness of the arguments of Pacific Northwest residents, and the fact they did not possess the national banking capital to subscribe the four million dollar capital required for a Federal Reserve Bank, meant that one large Pacific Coast district was created under the leadership of San Francisco. The committee concluded that a weak bank in a borrowing region (the Pacific Northwest) "would not offer the cheerful possibilities that a large bank with branches could extend--the large bank located at San Francisco to embrace the entire coast."[56] In accordance with Section 3 of the Federal Reserve Act, Federal Reserve Bank branches were opened at Spokane, Seattle, and Portland in 1917, at Salt Lake City in 1918, and at Los Angeles in 1920 to handle the "distinct types of paper (which) grew out of the different types of business activity in those areas."[57] However, the parent branch--the Federal Reserve Bank at San Francisco--still retained final authority over rediscounting of paper at all branches. Consequently, even though the primacy of San Francisco had not gone unchallenged, the city and the bank directors of San Francisco still retained significant authority over economic activity in the Pacific Northwest and the Great Basin well into the twentieth century.

NOTES

1. See Lamoreaux, "Banks, Kinship, and Economic Development: The New England Case," *Journal of Economic History* 46 (September 1986).
2. Nash, *State Government and Economic Development* 29-30.
3. James Hunter, *Partners in Progress 1864-1950: A Brief History of the Bank of California* (New York: The Newcomen Society, 1950), 28.
4. Dana, *The Man Who Built San Francisco*, 175. In particular, Ralston's partners were disgruntled at a loan Ralston made to Captain John Ainsworth, founder of the Oregon Steam Navigation Company. See Neil Wilson, *400 California Street* (San Francisco: The Bank of California, 1964), 13-15.
5. The National Bank Act was interpreted to prohibit branching; many states were hostile to branch banking. Eugene White [*The Regulation and Reform of the American Banking System, 1900-1929* (Princeton: Princeton University Press, 1983), 15] shows that in 1909, only ten states allowed limited branch banking. California allowed statewide branching.
6. See the detailed histories of Wells, Fargo and Company by Turrentine W. Jackson: *Wells Fargo & Co. in Idaho Territory* (Boise: Idaho State Historical Society, 1984); "Portland: Wells Fargo's Hub for the Pacific Northwest," *Oregon Historical Quarterly* (Fall 1985); and "Salt Lake City: Wells Fargo's Transportation Depot during the Stagecoach Era," *Utah Historical Quarterly* 53 (Winter 1985).
7. This was amended in 1862 and again in 1864 to allow the incorporation of savings and commercial banks.
8. Quoted in Noel Loomis, *Wells Fargo* (New York: Clarkson Potter, 1968), 6.
9. See Jackson, "Portland", and "Salt Lake City".
10. See Loomis, *Wells Fargo*, 237. Joseph Crumb, "Banking Regulation in California" (Ph.D. diss., University of California, 1935), however, dates the charter of the Wells Fargo banking business in California as 1866.
11. Jackson, "Portland," 260.
12. Cross, *Financing an Empire*, 540.
13. Cross, *Financing an Empire*, 540.

14. Loomis, *Wells Fargo*, 288. This is interesting, since Wells Fargo Bank is one of the largest branched banks in the United States today.
15. This had the beneficial effect for Wells Fargo of, in essence, requiring borrowers to maintain compensating balances at the bank.
16. It is not surprising that these railroads received funding; two of the stockholders of Wells Fargo were Leland Stanford and Charles Crocker.
17. Loomis, *Wells Fargo*, 239-246.
18. Loomis, *Wells Fargo*, 252-254.
19. Loomis, *Wells Fargo*, 173.
20. Loomis, *Wells Fargo*, 225.
21. Nash, *State Government and Economic Development*, 89-91.
22. The head office was in Sacramento, where Stanford and Huntington had their start as merchants.
23. Code, "Spatial Dynamics of Financial Intermediaries," 292, suggests that the rapid acquisition of information is less of a locational determinant for insurance companies, probably because the assets they purchase are long-term in nature. As a result, these companies made inroads into the West earlier than other intermediaries.
24. Bruce Pritchett, *A Study of Capital Mobilization: The Life Insurance Industry of the Nineteenth Century* (New York: Arno Press, 1977), 236.
25. See U.S. Bureau of the Census, *Report on Insurance Business in the United States* (Washington, D.C.: Government Printing Office, 1895), Eleventh Census, volume 12, part II.
26. C.I.D. Moore, *The Pacific Mutual Life Insurance Company of California* (Los Angeles: Pacific Mutual Life Insurance Company, 1928), 43.
27. Moore, *Pacific Mutual Life Insurance Company*, 72. I would argue that the primacy of San Francisco was established long before 1880, but that inertia and tradition had kept the company's headquarters in Sacramento long past that city's ability to attract or retain business.
28. Moore, *Pacific Mutual Life Insurance Company*, 87, 186.

29. Moore, *Pacific Mutual Life Insurance Company*, 185-186. 1877 legislation in California limited the investments of life insurance companies to federal, state, or local government bonds, or "local" real estate. The definition of "local" in this case seems to have been "regional."
30. Moore, *Pacific Mutual Life Insurance Company*, 107-114.
31. Moore, *Pacific Mutual Life Insurance Company*, 116.
32. Robert Cleland and Frank Putnam, *Isaias W. Hellman and the Farmers and Merchants Bank* (San Marino, California: The Huntington Library, 1965) 8.
33. See Leroy Armstrong and J.O. Denny, *Financial California* (San Francisco: Coast Banker Publishing, 1916), 157-158; Joseph King, *History of the San Francisco Stock and Exchange Board* (San Francisco: J.L. King, 1910), 3-4.
34. James Walter, *The Role of Regional Security Exchanges* (Berkeley: University of California Press, 1957), 11-12.
35. Vance, *Geography and Urban Evolution*, 18-20.
36. The personal papers of William Chapman Ralston at the Bancroft Library of the University of California include stacks of such encoded telegrams.
37. King, *San Francisco Stock and Exchange Board*, 78.
38. Parker B. Willis, *The Federal Reserve Bank of San Francisco* (New York: Columbia University Press, 1937), 78.
39. Quoted in Pomeroy, *Pacific Slope*, 127.
40. Willis, *Federal Reserve Bank of San Francisco*, 262-263. At least nine Southern Pacific Railroad bonds were listed.
41. James, *Money and Capital Markets*, 89-148.
42. Sylla, "Federal Policy, Banking Market Structure," 680-681.
43. Mr. Philip Forstall of Rand McNally Co., was very helpful in locating and duplicating copies of the directory not available in libraries.
44. See Michael Conzen, "The Maturing Urban System in the United States, 1840-1910," *Annals of the Association of American Geographers* 67 (March 1977), 88-108.
45. Willis, *Federal Reserve Bank of San Francisco*, 80.
46. John James ["The Evolution of the National Money Market 1888-1911" (Ph.D. diss., MIT, 1974), 168] finds that San Francisco dominated its region in holding correspondent balances more than any other city dominated its region, with

the exception of New York City in the Middle Atlantic, and Boston in New England.

47. The figures on bank correspondent choices may be biased upward somewhat, since some banks chose more than one correspondent in a city. This bias would be stronger in the figures for New York City and Chicago, with large numbers of banks in each city, than for San Francisco where there were a more limited number of possible correspondents.

48. U.S. Congress, Senate, *Banking and Currency Hearings on HR7837: Bill to Provide for Establishment of Federal Reserve Banks* (63rd Cong., 1st sess. S.Doc 232, 1913), 113.

49. U.S. Congress, Senate Federal Bank Organization Committee, *Letter to the Federal Reserve Board Relative to the Location of the Federal Reserve Banks* (63rd Cong., 2nd sess., S.Doc 485, 1914), 357.

50. Federal Bank Organization Committee, *Letter*, 365.

51. Willis, *Federal Reserve Bank of San Francisco*, 96.

52. Willis, *Federal Reserve Bank of San Francisco*, 87.

53. Willis, *Federal Reserve Bank of San Francisco*, 91.

54. Willis, *Federal Reserve Bank of San Francisco*, 89-91.

55. Federal Bank Organization Committee, *Letter*, 336.

56. Willis, *Federal Reserve Bank of San Francisco*, 90.

57. Willis, *Federal Reserve Bank of San Francisco*, 105.

CHAPTER 6

Testing the Market Integration Hypothesis

Measurement of the quantity and direction of capital flows within the Pacific Coast region would be ideal data for an analysis of the scope of financial markets. Unfortunately, the difficulties associated with input-output or flow-of-funds techniques are large even when data is abundant.[1] The sophistication and accuracy of data required for such techniques precludes any application to historical periods when data is scarce. At best, histories of individual investors and savers, as presented in previous chapters, can only hint at the direction of capital flows.

While the measurement of actual capital flows is troublesome, we can gauge the financial market within the Pacific Coast region by observing price behavior, particularly interest rates and asset prices. That is, while individual demand and supply curves comprising a market are unknown, the level and movement of the price of loanable funds will be determined by these underlying market forces. Thus, the comparison of the prices of funds at different locations can tell us about the power of those market forces. If the prices of funds are identical and move together in two locations, it is strong evidence (barring the remote possibility of pure coincidence) that the same market coordinates requirements for and supplies of investable funds at the two points. Figure 6.1 lists the markets tested, and their abbreviations. (All Figures cited can be found in the Appendix.)

In order to make a statistical analysis possible and relatively simple, I divide the market into three arbitrary segments: the market for very short-term funds (commercial funds used to move goods or crops), the market for long-term funds (mortgages), and the market for "medium-term" funds lent for periods generally longer than a few months but less than three years.[2] In a world of fully developed financial markets, these three segments would be interlinked. The economist would characterize such connections with a model of a term structure of interest rates, in which rates on an asset of one maturity reflect rates on assets of all other maturities and expectations about future interest rates. The evidence on such fully integrated markets is questionable today[3] and little work has been done on its applicability in the past.[4] However, since the present concern is with the geographical mobility of funds, it is only necessary in this research to compare interest rates on relatively homogeneous assets differentiated only by the location of borrower.

THE SHORT-TERM MONEY MARKET

The short-term money market was primarily organized to facilitate the movement of goods and crops. Loans in this case were of short duration--from a few days in some commercial transactions or from three to six months for crop production and marketing. In either case, the loans were usually backed by the commodities in question. Loans with this kind of collateral are the "self-liquidating" loan type central to the classical real bills approach to banking. In 1925, Allyn Young undertook a study of the seasonal movements of national bank deposits and loans associated with agricultural production in the different regions of the United States.[5] It is interesting that he singled out only four cities for use in comparing regional cycles to financial center cycles: New York City, Boston, Chicago, and San Francisco. At that time, cities acted as regional financial centers and were called upon to help finance crop planting in spring and harvest in autumn. They were also depositories of excess funds from the hinterland in slack periods of winter and summer.[6]

The Rand McNally correspondent information cited in Chapter 5 makes it clear that San Francisco acted as financier of agricultural needs in the Far West. Young's analysis of national banks between 1901 and 1913 confirms that San Francisco provided for the seasonal needs of the Pacific Coast region.[7] In Figure 6.2a, we can see that movements in individual deposits less clearinghouse exchanges in San

Francisco mimic (with typically wider swings) the movements in the Pacific Coast states. Figure 6.2b shows a similarly close relationship between San Francisco and the Pacific Coast states in seasonal movements of loans and discounts, with a peak for both series during the harvest in the autumn, and a trough during the slack winter season. San Francisco's relationship to the Pacific Coast region appears very much like Boston's relationship to New England. Both cities act as financial centers for their respective regions.[8] This is hardly surprising considering the centralization of shipping, processing, and warehousing services in San Francisco.

Short-term capital was also in demand to finance the shipment of goods. This need was frequently met by the issuance of commercial paper--short-term notes backed by the commodities themselves. These notes had specialized brokers in the eastern United States as early as 1800; the brokers were able to transact business over long distances with well-known firms. The bank correspondent system aided the dispersion of such paper when banks in cities acted as agents in the purchase of commercial paper for their correspondents in the hinterland.

Commercial paper rates on these short-term bills were frequently quoted in newspapers and financial journals of the nineteenth century and many large cities had active secondary markets.[9] Local paper dealers had established themselves on the Pacific Coast by 1900, and branches of national commercial paper houses were opened in San Francisco by 1908 and in Seattle by 1910; their appearance in Portland occurred later.[10] Davis cites the spread of such commercial paper houses nationwide as a stimulant to capital flows and an indication of the integration of regional capital markets.[11]

We know that in 1931, San Francisco had a commercial paper house with formal branches in Seattle, Spokane, Tacoma, Portland, Oakland, San Jose, and Los Angeles.[12] This branching was informally in place many years earlier; since the sale of commercial paper required knowledge of firms and since the paper usually backed commercial transactions, the regionality of business in the Pacific Coast region would lead to regionality of commercial paper financing. However, the evidence on commercial paper rates as a measure of market integration on the Pacific Coast is meager. Bradstreet's correspondents reported local commercial paper rates on quality paper,[13] but the coverage of the Pacific Coast region in this journal was sporadic and ranges were more often quoted than were exact rates as was typical for New York City or Chicago. Figure 6.3 gives an indication of the manner in which rates were reported in *Bradstreet's Journal*.[14] At best, from this type of data we establish that San Francisco rates were lower than other Pacific Coast region rates and that rates in general declined in the nineteenth century. However a well-specified functional relationship cannot be calculated.

THE MORTGAGE MARKET

At the other end of the spectrum was the mortgage market. There, funds were lent on real estate collateral. The Census Office for the Census of 1890 made a special report on mortgages in that year, no doubt in response to the growing political unrest among the nation's farmers. In that extensive report, mortgage data on lots (urban real estate, usually) and on acres (agricultural real estate) were collected by special agents from public mortgage records in county real estate record offices. Based on these records, the agents calculated average annual rates charged on new mortgages entered in each year between 1880 and 1889 in each state and in 28 of the largest cities. The agents were careful to include additional commissions (points) that borrowers were obliged to pay (especially in Western and North Central states) in order to obtain the true costs of borrowing.

Figures 6.4a-6.4m present data on lot and acre mortgage rates for New York City, Chicago, Illinois, San Francisco, and the Pacific Coast states. As is clear, Pacific Coast rates exceeded the San Francisco rate by a large amount, and the San Francisco rate exceeded the New York City rate. Census officials noted that mortgage rates "show a pretty closely corresponding increase westward." But, the "progress is broken. . .by California, because it is not geographically situated in the order of settlement."[15] More to the point than order of settlement (since Oregon settlement predates California) is that San Francisco was a sophisticated financial center which had learned how to recycle funds before any other western or southern city. The differentials we see in mortgage rates have been attributed to differential risk of mortgages in the hinterlands versus the centers and of the West versus the East.[16] Census officials also recognized that differential costs of collection and foreclosure contributed to interest rate differentials. A reading of the history of financial development suggests that east-west rate differentials were probably more a function of market segmentation than of risk premiums.[17]

Do the rates fluctuate together as capital scarcity in one state stimulates a capital outflow from (and an interest rate increase in) another market? Is there correlation of rate movements over time? Simple correlation coefficients calculated for the interest rates in various locations are presented in Table 6.1. As a benchmark, consider the relationship between lot mortgage rates in Chicago versus lot mortgage rates in Illinois.[18] Clearly, with a correlation coefficient of 0.989, there was a very close correspondence of rate movements in Chicago and its downstate hinterland. There was a less close correlation between rates in the two largest urban areas of Chicago and New York City; this is not particularly surprising, given the propensity for local speculative activity in urban real estate. Somewhat surprising is the correlation coefficient of 0.881 between lot rates in New York City and lot rates in San Francisco. However, several authors have suggested that inflows of eastern funds into the Pacific Coast region were most likely to be in the form of long-term debt.[19] The connection of San Francisco to Washington is close, with the coefficient equal to 0.846; this is consistent with the historical evidence on the large influx of San Francisco capital into Washington's urban areas such as Seattle and Tacoma. The relationship is less close between slow-growing Oregon and San Francisco. The lower coefficient between San Francisco and California may be a result of the late 1880s real estate boom in Los Angeles which was financed by both local funds from the newly-developing local financial center and funds of new immigrants from the eastern states.[20]

To get a grasp on the relationship between urban and rural mortgage markets, Table 6.1 also presents the correlation coefficient between the rates on lots in city centers and rates on acres in states. The correlations here tend to be higher than the correlations between urban mortgage rates, which runs counter to some economic geographers' assumption that cities are better connected to each other than they are to rural areas. This assumption is probably incorrect, at least insofar as these simple correlations go, since there was a tendency for urban areas to experience local and brief speculative booms which were less likely to occur in agricultural areas. The speculative nature of these booms might tend to inhibit the normal function of financial markets in arbitraging interest differentials. Thus Los Angeles experienced sharp swings in rates during the real estate boom, which

TABLE 6.1

CORRELATION COEFFICIENTS FOR MORTGAGE RATES

Rate on Lots		Rate on Acres	
NYC, CHI	= +0.777	-------------------	
NYC, SFO	= +0.881	-------------------	
CHI, SFO	= +0.800	-------------------	
NYC, NY	= +0.999	NYC, NY	= +0.968
CHI, IL	= +0.989	CHI, IL	= +0.878
SFO, CA	= +0.684	SFO, CA	= +0.930
SFO, OR	= + 0.682	SFO, OR	= +0.922
SFO, WA	= +0.846	SFO, WA	= +0.711

NOTES: Data are annual average rates on new mortgages made on property in each location in each year, 1880–1889, from U.S. Bureau of the Census, *Report on Real Estate Mortgages in the U.S. at the Eleventh Census* (Washington, D.C., Government Printing Office, 1895), 249–251.

For city rates used in calculating the correlation of rates on acres, the rate on mortgages made on lots was used, since no mortgage rates on acres in cities were reported.

caused its rates to diverge from San Francisco's,[21] while the rest of California was moving along at a more normal pace, and borrowing for mortgages (a large part of which came from San Francisco, according to Doti[22]) did not change radically in this ten-year period. The lower correlation between San Francisco lot rates and Washington acres rates suggests that, if money flowed from San Francisco, it was more likely to go to urban mortgages than into agricultural mortgages. This is consistent with some amount of risk aversion or some differentially high transactions costs associated with agricultural areas in Washington versus urban areas in that state.

How were these mortgage funds mobilized? Unlike the farm states of Illinois, Kansas, Nebraska, and Iowa studied by Bogue, mortgage companies do not appear to have been numerous or powerful mobilizers of mortgage funds in the Pacific Coast region.[23] This may be partly due to the uncertain status of land titles in California during the 1850s and 1860s. The 1851 federal court decision and Act of Congress honoring all Mexican land grants in the state set the precedents for years of litigation by opposing claimants to plots of land in the state.[24] Consequently, companies selling shares of mortgage portfolios were at a disadvantage because it was difficult to ascertain which party had clear title to the land.

Banks, however, were not similarly disadvantaged. Local presence gave them both better information on borrowers and the ability to closely monitor loans. Thus, state-chartered banks in San Francisco were lending on real estate across the state as early as the 1870s.[25] In fact, California savings banks were required to hold 50 percent of their real estate loans on land located in California.[26] It is likely that some of the rest of the mortgage portfolio consisted of loans to other states in the Pacific region. An examination of California state banking reports shows that San Francisco banks were lending on real estate as far away as Arizona and New Mexico, but that the bulk of out-of-state loans appears to have been made in Oregon and Washington. Table 6.2 lists the totals for loans made on real estate collateral by non-national banks in California between 1878 and 1908. The percentage of loans for which collateral was located in Oregon and Washington reached a peak in 1893, when more than seven percent of all real estate loans were made on Pacific Northwest collateral. Over time this percentage gradually declined; only 1.2 percent of real estate loans were made on collateral located in Oregon and Washington in 1908.

Severe limitations were placed on the real estate mortgage portfolios that national banks were allowed to hold. Banks in central reserve cities (New York City, Chicago, and St. Louis) were forbidden to make real estate loans. Other national banks were permitted to take real estate as collateral on existing loans up to five years in length, provided each loan was for an amount less than fifty percent of the appraised value of the land; total real estate loans could not exceed 25 percent of the bank's capital. Despite these prohibitions, it is clear that national banks made some real estate loans. Census officials in 1890 noted that national banks circumvented usury limits by contracting in the names of their officers; it is possible that loan limitations could be similarly evaded.

Keehn and Smiley find that the supposed prohibition of real estate mortgages could be evaded, when "borrower and lender . . . agreed to an unsecured loan with the understanding that it would be renewed with a mortgage note as security."[27] Given the propensity of Pacific Coast banks for loan renewal[28] it is quite likely that such mortgage provisions were instituted, making national banks, in effect, participants in the long-term capital market. In 1911, the Comptroller of the Currency found that 1.5 percent of California's national bank loans, 2.2 percent of Oregon's and 2.6 percent of Washington's were loans secured directly by mortgages.[29] These figures are higher than for all Eastern and many Old South states. Keehn and Smiley also find that throughout the years between 1890 and 1913, the ratio of real estate held (including real estate taken in foreclosure and real estate directly or indirectly backing loans) to loans and discounts was higher in the Pacific Coast states than anywhere outside the farming belt of the central United States and the Mountain West.[30]

THE NATIONAL BANKING SYSTEM

Since the National Bank Act of 1864 (which superseded the original Bank Act of 1863), a dual banking system consisting of both nationally-chartered and state-chartered banks has characterized the United States. National banks were subject to uniform regulations concerning capital requirements, loan provisions, and financial reporting. In general, these banks had higher capital requirements and somewhat more restrictive loan provisions than banks chartered under

TABLE 6.2

VALUE OF LOANS MADE BY
CALIFORNIA NON-NATIONAL BANKS
ON REAL ESTATE COLLATERAL LOCATED IN
OREGON AND WASHINGTON

Year	Total Real Estate Loans Made	Value of Loans Made with Collateral of OR or WA Real Estate	Percent of Total Real Estate Loans w/ OR or WA Collateral
1878	$ 66,535,201	$ 0	0
1883	$ 66,071,781	$ 12,748	0.02%
1888	$ 67,227,232	$ 1,003,090	1.49%
1893	$129,242,741	$ 9,365,800	7.25%
1899	$107,104,395	$ 4,963,949	4.63%
1905	$177,658,943	$ 4,491,308	2.53%
1908	$212,921,077	$ 2,490,690	1.17%

NOTES: All data are from the *Annual Report* of the California State Banking Commission, for June 1878, January 1883, July 1888, July 1893, July 1899, August 1905, and March 1908.

Non-national banks include state-chartered savings banks, commercial banks, foreign-chartered banks, and private banks. Loans were classified by location of collateral real estate only when that location was clearly stated.

the different state statutes. Because of the more relaxed regulation of state banking authorities, few western banks converted their charters to national bank status immediately following the enactment in 1864. Consequently, in 1865 a law was passed which would place taxes on note issue of state banks; the aim was to reduce state bank profitability and to force them to take out national charters. The result was a dramatic decline in the number of state banks nationwide, from 1089 state banks in 1864 to 349 in 1865. State banks remained at a disadvantage until the rise of the (non-taxable) checking deposit in the 1880s; the number of state banks then increased until it equalled the number of national banks in 1895.[31]

In the Pacific Coast states, national banks were originally at a disadvantage because their notes were not convertible into gold--the medium of exchange on the Coast.[32] Congress authorized the chartering of National Gold Banks in 1870, as a means of drawing western banks, dependent upon metallic specie, into the national bank system.[33] The first national bank, a national gold bank, was chartered in California in 1871. With the resumption of convertibility in 1879, the distinction between national banks and national gold banks disappeared. State banks continued to flourish, especially in California. Table 6.3 presents comparisons of the relative size of state commercial and national banks in the Pacific Coast region. Throughout the late nineteenth and early twentieth centuries, national banks dominated state banks in the Pacific Northwest where state prohibition of bank note issue gave national banks a competitive edge. National banks were slower to assert themselves in California, which had created a large state bank system based on specie prior to the enactment of the National Bank Act in 1864.

It is important to note that the larger average size of national banks (because of their higher capital requirements), the formalized network established between national banks (because of their reserve arrangements with reserve agents and correspondents), and the prestige and visibility of national bank status allowed national banks to have important influence on the flow of funds. The national bank charter may have given those banks a trustworthy image, attracting depositors

TABLE 6.3
AGGREGATE ASSETS AND LIABILITIES OF BANKS
IN THE PACIFIC COAST REGION
($ millions)

	Loans	Deposits	Capital	#	Loans	Deposits	Capital	#
	California State Banks				California National Banks			
1888	69	48	40	110	20	18	8	39
1893	85	47	48	173	16	11	8	32
1896	76	57	41	174	18	17	8	31
1898	74	67	31	176	25	28	11	34
1902	96	118	29	187	43	51	12	49
1907	182	199	49	339	135	133	29	126
1908	154	165	47	355	125	124	34	139
1911	109	119	31	315	225	217	52	203
1913	120	140	32	406	272	258	56	252
	Oregon State Banks				Oregon National Banks			
1888	na	na	na	na	6	5	2	25
1893	0.8	0.4	0.6	12	11	9	4	39
1896	0.9	0.6	0.8	15	7	7	3	33
1898	2	3	1	18	5	9	2	29
1902	3	5	0.9	18	9	16	2	30
1907	19	28	4	96	25	34	4	53
1908	26	42	7	132	23	34	4	63
1911	24	31	6	143	37	47	7	77
1913	26	28	6	140	46	55	9	83
	Washington State Banks				Washington National Banks			
1888	na	na	na	na	5	5	2	23
1893	8	7	4	64	15	9	7	64
1896	0.8	0.8	0.5	14	8	7	5	41
1898	2	3	0.6	15	7	13	4	33
1902	7	13	1	40	18	30	3	34
1907	23	26	3	84	50	60	6	41
1908	45	66	11	196	46	61	8	62
1911	36	42	7	206	65	80	12	80
1913	42	49	9	231	73	87	12	77

Notes: # = number of banks. All data are from U.S. Comptroller of the Currency *Annual Reports*, which compiled figures reported from state banking authorities. The returns for state banks in Oregon and Washington are unofficial until 1907. State bank figures do not include chartered savings banks, which were numerous in California. National bank figures are for the fourth call of the year, and include reserve city returns; state bank figures are for reported date of examination.

and capital from outside the bank's immediate vicinity. George Barnett believes that

> in one respect. . .the state banks, even in those States in which the regulation and supervision is of a high order, are at a disadvantage as compared with the national banks. Where there are relations between a person or a bank in one State and a bank in another, especially in a distant State, the state bank suffers in competition with the national banks, since in most cases the citizens of one State are not acquainted with the merits of the banking laws of another State, whereas they know the general character of the national bank act.[34]

The Comptroller of the Currency (the administrator of all national banks in the country) required uniform financial practices and reports from all banks with national charters. Thus, balance sheets were submitted on five call dates each year and income statements were submitted twice yearly. In contrast, the reporting practices of state chartered banks were spotty, inconsistent, and non-existent at early dates.[35] California state banks were required, beginning in 1878, to submit yearly balance sheets but income statements were published only for state savings banks. Oregon and Washington state banks did not submit official balance sheets until after 1909. Consequently, attempts to compare the financial activities of Pacific Coast region state-chartered banks is very difficult. On the other hand, the national bank balance sheets are comprehensive enough to separate non-earning assets (bank building, furniture etc) from earning assets (loans, bonds, stocks). Income statements report net earnings semi-annually from 1869 to 1911, and gross earnings, expenses, and losses semi-annually from 1888 to 1911. Sample balance sheet and income statement formats are presented in Figure 6.5.

NATIONAL BANK INTEREST RATES

With measures of earnings and earning assets, we can calculate the realized rates of return earned by national banks in different locations on the Pacific Coast. While income statements were not published on a bank-by-bank basis, earning figures are available for non-reserve city banks ("country banks") aggregated to the state level, and for reserve city banks aggregated to the city level. Clearly, much detail is lost in this aggregation, but attention to this data would be an improvement upon earlier works which aggregated these figures into arbitrary regional totals.[36] For the purposes of studying the connection of hinterland areas to financial centers, the Comptroller data seem to provide the best available uniform series covering the period of rapid extensive and intensive growth in the Pacific Coast region.

In order to create a series of the greatest length, Lance Davis calculated the ratio of net earnings to earning assets in his important work of 1965. He argued that net rates could be regarded as proxies for movements in the levels of average interest rates since he expected operating expenses to be constant between regions and years.[37] However, subsequent studies have suggested that operating expenses were not constant and that Davis' net earning rates do not track actual interest rates very closely.[38] Since this research is concerned with the market's determination of rates on financial assets rather than on the ex post net return realized by investors, it is the gross earning rates that form the data set for the empirical work here.

The James Series

This book uses a gross-earnings series developed by John James.[39] James was concerned that the simple ratio of gross or net earnings to total assets originally proposed by Davis was not an accurate representation of the rate *charged* by national banks on their loans. Instead, it represented average earnings on a portfolio of very diverse assets, including loans and discounts, bonds, correspondent balances, and so on. Since these are heterogeneous assets, the average of interest earned on them has no real economic meaning. Assets such as United States bonds were traded nationally, so returns on those were uniform across the country, while loans and discounts were traded or negotiated in smaller, more local markets. James reasoned that, if earnings attributed to non-loan assets could be determined and subtracted from gross earnings, the resulting total could be assumed to be earned from interest charges on loans and discounts alone.[40] Thus, the rate derived by James will reflect conditions relevant to the loan and discount market alone, and the size of this market can be judged by looking at the relationships among rates on loans negotiated by banks in different locations.

James' rates were calculated semi-annually in the following way:

$$R_t = \frac{[GE_t - r_{us}(BC+BD)_t - r_{BB}DB_t - r_{RRB}OSB_t]}{[(L+D)_{t-1} - LS_t]}$$

where

R = bank earning rate on loans loans, calculated semi-annually

GE = gross earnings

r_{US} = average rate on US bonds held

BC = dollar value of bonds held to back note circulation

BD = dollar value of bonds held to back public deposits

r_{BB} = rate paid on bankers' balances

DB = dollar value of bankers' balances owned

r_{RRB} = average yield on railroad bonds

OSB = dollar value of stocks and non-US bonds

L+D = dollar value of loans and discounts

LS = dollar value of loans charged off

These rates were calculated for each reserve city and for each state's country banks. The semi-annual periods to 1906 are September to March and March to September; thus, the first semi-annual rate (designated 1888:1) actually covers earnings from September 1887 to March 1888. From 1906 to 1911, the periods are January to July and

July to January.[41] Balance sheet items such as loans and discounts were reported at five call dates per year, so James interpolates, then averages between calls to acheive semi-annual averages on these items.[42]

Since the rate received by national banks on U.S. bonds was the same nationwide, these earnings were deducted, using the dollar amount of such bonds held and an average yield on U.S. securities held which was calculated by the Comptroller. James finds that the rate of interest earned on bankers' balances held in New York City remained nearly constant at 2 percent throughout the period, so he uses this rate to deduct earnings from a bank's deposits held with a correspondent. Finally, Macaulay's index of yields on railroad bonds (unadjusted series) is used to calculate earnings on other stocks and bonds. James supports this method by pointing out that in 1908, railroad bonds made up 66 percent of non-government bond holdings at national banks.[43]

The residual earnings thus derived are attributed to the bank's loan and discount portfolio. In order to achieve the closest proxy to the stated rate (the rate actually charged customers, as opposed to the rate eventually received by the bank), James creates a figure for the loans which actually paid interest. He contends that most loans were about six months in length, so that loans made in period t-1 were realized in period t.[44] Also, loan defaults were written off as losses, presumably in the same six month period in which they were supposed to have been paid.[45] Thus, the "performing" loan and discount portfolio which produces earnings in period t consists of $[(L+D)_{t-1}-LS_t]$. James compares his interest rate proxies to a Comptroller series of rates charged by banks in 1902, and to a number of Bradstreet commercial paper series, and is satisfied that his rates were representative of average interest rates charged by banks.

The great advantage in these rates is their consistency over a long period of time and over a wide geographical area. Since the comparison of these rates occurs within one banking system governed by uniform regulations and reporting requirements, the resulting conclusions should be representative of the impact of geographical variations (rather than variations in bank regulation) on capital mobility. Furthermore, the rates are short-term, and should quickly reflect changes in credit conditions, which is an improvement over the use of long-term mortgage or bond rates.

There are no clear biases or problems inherent in this system that would distort the derivation of Pacific Coast rates. Since this series uses national bank data alone, state banks' behavior in the financial market is not directly reflected. This is more of a problem for California, where state commercial and savings banks created the majority of loans and discounts, than it is for Oregon and Washington. It is not clear, however, that state banks should have or would have offered consistently different interest rates than national banks.

The use of the average United States bond rate earned by national banks across the country is not apparently problematic; there is no reason to suspect that Coast banks held U.S. bonds with different coupons than the rest of the country held. The rate earned on bankers' balances, assumed by James to be two percent, may differ in the Pacific Coast region. James apparently believes that competition for correspondent balances was nationwide, so that the New York City rate was the average rate also earned by deposits held in other cities. The Rand McNally data cited in Chapter 5 shows that Pacific Coast region banks did have many New York correspondents, so that the competition for balances could have been strong enough to create a uniform national rate. If there is a bias here, it would likely be not that the individual Pacific Coast states each faced a different rate on correspondent balances (thus, the constant two percent rule would mask regional variation in earnings), but that they all faced the same, possibly higher, rate paid by San Francisco banks, the destination of many correspondent balances. Thus, James' calculated rates would all be biased upward by deducting too little earnings on correspondent balances, but the rates would not be affected differentially by his assumption.

Finally, James assumes that the larger part of "other stocks and bonds" is nationally-traded railroad stocks, and he uses Macaulay's series to determine earnings on them. It is quite possible that local stocks were held by Pacific Coast national banks; state banks certainly held such securities. But, since "other stocks and bonds" represented only a fraction of total earning assets, the error introduced by this assumption should be small.

Comparing James' Series to Other Series

Graphs of the rates derived by James are presented in Figures 6.6a-6.6j. The very volatile nature of the rates, as may be expected on banking assets, is evident around the general long-term trend for rates over the period 1888-1911. For comparative purposes, Figure 6.7 shows James' New York City rate with an index of industrial stock yields and Macaulay's railroad bond yield index. The bank earning rates are in general lower than the industrial stock yields, as might be expected given the relative youth of the industrial stock markets. The bank rate is also more volatile than railroad stock yields, which is normal given the greater thickness of the railroad securities market.[46] For reasons mentioned earlier, it is difficult to compare the James series on Pacific Coast region rates to alternative series: there are no comparable series on Pacific Coast stock and bond data, which is the reason for using the James series. The Bradstreet's commercial paper rates collected earlier give little indication of variability since the rates are quoted in ranges.

There is a two year overlap in the Census mortgage series and the James series. Table 6.4 compares the bank earning rate to the rate on lot mortgages and on acre mortgages in 1888 and 1889. Both bank rates and mortgage rates tend to rise as the distance from San Francisco increases. What is interesting is that James' rates at times exceed the quoted mortgage rates. Although one normally expects liquidity preference to cause long-term interest rates to exceed short-term rates, the deflation which characterized the United States until 1897 may have been embodied in a downward-sloping term structure, where short-term rates exceeded long-term rates. However, the rather distinct markets of bank assets and of mortgage assets make comparison, especially over only two years, not particularly meaningful. The national bank earning rates, while admittedly imperfect, are geographically and temporally consistent. Given the lack of similarly consistent series on other interest rates outside the eastern financial centers, these bank rates can be used to give an idea of the integration of short-term financial markets during the period of rapid growth and development on the Pacific Coast.

TABLE 6.4

COMPARISON OF ANNUAL BANK AND MORTGAGE RATES
(annual percentages)

	James' Bank Rate	Census Mortgage Rates On Lots	On Acres
SFO, 1888	6.65	6.58	----
SFO, 1889	7.60	6.61	----
CA, 1888	8.14	8.88	8.99
CA, 1889	8.81	8.45	9.03
OR, 1888	9.01	9.63	9.44
OR, 1889	7.94	9.64	9.28
WA, 1888	11.35	9.70	9.49
WA, 1889	10.93	9.27	8.00

NOTES: James' Bank Rate data are taken from John James, "The Evolution of the National Money Market" (Ph.D. diss., MIT, 1974). Census Mortgage Rate data are taken from U.S. Census Office, *Report on Real Estate Mortgages in the United States at the Eleventh Census: 1890* (Washington, D.C., Government Printing Office, 1895), 248–251.

James' semi–annual series was arithmetically averaged into one year periods, extending from September of year t–1 to September of year t.

Rate Differentials versus Covariability

All of the standard works on national capital market integration (Davis, Sylla, Smiley, and James) have couched their analysis in terms of the reduction of interest differentials between regions in the United States.[47] In these sorts of analyses, it is assumed that geographically separate capital markets are integrated when interest rates are the same across space. But as George Stigler pointed out in response to Davis' 1965 article, price (or interest rate) differentials alone do not necessarily indicate market imperfections or segmentation since the market may be correctly pricing higher risk, uncertainty, or cost involved in particular transactions occurring in different locations.[48]

The difficulty in the differentials approach, especially using bank earning rates, is that it is not clear (and, in fact, is probably not true) that the same riskiness, uncertainty, and transaction costs are involved in making bank loans in different parts of the country. Thus, an interest differential between, New York City and Seattle, may not reflect segmentation so much as higher risks and uncertainty associated with economic activity in Seattle, or higher information costs of making loans in distant areas. In a strict sense, interest rates should only be equal on financial instruments having exactly the same characteristics such as borrower risk, monitoring cost, search cost, and so on. But bank loans are likely to differ greatly with respect to these characteristics, especially for loans made in locations distant from each other. In fact, "loan and mortgage contracts are among the most heterogeneous of credit instruments in financial markets."[49]

Without careful measurements of the effect of different risk and costs on bank rates, a measurement of interest differentials alone will not be an accurate reflection of geographical market segmentation, nor will the reduction of those differentials alone represent the integration of those markets. While we might expect the reduction of differentials to occur as technological improvements lower transactions and information costs, and as geographical diversification of portfolios reduces risk premiums, the absolute size of the differential at a point in time and the changing size of the differential over time can not completely summarize the state of market segmentation or integration.[50]

Instead of looking only at the size and reduction of differentials, the research presented here considers the degree of similarity in movements of the bank rates over the period. Most current work on capital market integration considers covariability to be a stronger test of integration than the size or movement of differentials. Davis, although employing the differentials approach in his 1965 work, later acknowledged that "if markets are closely linked, external stimuli in one should produce adjustments in both; but if they are not so tied, such stimuli would affect one and not the other."[51] While making this statement, however, he used a simple "coefficient of concordance" test for regionally aggregated rates. These regionally aggregated rates do not have any behavioral significance unless regional homogeneity or market integration is already proven.

Sushka and Barrett seem to be the only economic historians who take up this consideration of relative covariance of interest rates as a measure of market integration (although they too focus on the causes of declining interest differentials as the main point of their research). They note that "a national or integrated market does not require identical prices but instead the existence of a behavioral relationship among markets." And, "if we observe a behavioral relationship between interest rates that suggests the presence of the communication of information between markets, we can conclude that a movement in one rate produces some appropriate movements in rates *in related markets*."[52] Sushka and Barrett, however, do not follow through on this analysis as completely as they could, relying on Davis' regionally-aggregated interest rate series.

For analysis of the degree of integration in the Pacific Coast region in this period, a log-linear specification of interest rate determination is used which, in its simplest form, appears as:

$$R_x = A{*}R_y^B$$

or, in logarithmic form,

$$log\, r_x = a + b\, log\, r_y$$

This is a convenient functional form in that we can gauge both the level of the interest rate differential between hinterland and center (this is captured by the coefficient *a* which measures the ratio of the two interest rates), as well as the sensitivity of hinterland rates to changes in the center rate, which is measured by the coefficient *b*, the elasticity between the two rates.[53] The logarithmic specification also has the advantage of automatically correcting for the heteroskedasticity which occurs when the variance of the data increases with the level of the data; Sushka and Barrett suggest this may occur when risk premiums rise or fall with interest rates.[54]

Intuitively, this functional form relates the demand and supply forces in each market, measured by R_x in each market. In a completely segmented market, R_x would be determined only by the local demands for and supplies of funds. In related markets, demands and supplies arising in other areas will also determine R_x as this rate responds to new inflows of funds from outside suppliers, or new outflows of funds to outside demanders. The effect of non-local demand and supply forces can be summarized by the interest rate R_y. Thus, while the level of interest rates may differ between the areas because of different transactions costs, the marginal movements in the rates should correspond if there is capital mobility between the areas.[55]

Can the coefficient *b* be correctly identified as a measure of sensitivity between hinterland and center which results from market connection? It is unlikely that pure coincidence would cause rates to fluctuate together over a twenty-five year period of rapid change in the United States. A more plausible alternative explanation for correspondence of rates would be that both rates are affected similarly by a third independent variable, such as national or regional business cycles. If this were the case, it would certainly tell us something about market integration, because it would suggest that the two areas under study were part of the same economic unit (in which the business cycle is occurring) or that there is a mechanism between the two areas which transmits local business fluctuations from one to another. This is, in fact, just another kind of market integration.[56]

A counterexample to this would be two isolated agricultural regions both hit by some natural catastrophe such as a drought. Even without a market existing between the two areas, the price of funds is likely to rise in both as farmers replant or borrow to carry them to the next harvest. In the analysis here, however, such an example is not particularly relevant since we are comparing the rates in outlying areas (more agricultural) to those in the financial center (more service-providing or industrial). Covariance of these rates due to a common natural disaster is unlikely. Transmission of local shocks from hinterland to center (or vice versa) will in this case be a matter of market connection, not coincidence.

Integration Benchmarks

In a world of perfectly integrated markets, equal transactions costs and risk premiums, and speedy translation of local shocks, the term *a* would equal zero (no interest differential) and the coefficient *b* would equal one (all current change in one rate is fully reflected in the other rate). In this case,

$$log\ r_x = 0 + 1*log\ r_y$$

Or, taking antilogs,

$$R_x = R_y$$

Given the heterogeneous nature of bank loans in general, and of national bank loan portfolios in particular, it would be surprising for any regional market to meet the stringent conditions of the term *a* equal to zero and the coefficient *b* equal to one.[57]

A less stringent and more reasonable approach would be to use coefficient benchmarks derived from regressions on developed Eastern areas--the areas of greatest capital market integration in this period, according to all sources. These benchmarks will measure "integration" as captured in national bank earning rates. Table 6.5 presents estimates of these benchmarks. To gauge highest integration two large and nearby centers in the East are chosen--New York City and Boston. The Boston rate is regressed on the New York City rate for the full period 1888 to 1911. As expected, the interest differential is very small, 0.141, and is not statistically different from zero. The sensitivity of Boston rates to New York City rates is very high, with the coefficient *b* equal to 0.741, which is not statistically different from one. Furthermore, the percentage of explained variance is relatively large, considering that there is only one explanatory variable. Movements in the New York City rate explain almost half of the variation in the Boston rate. Thus, the James series yields results consistent with the sort of relationship between developed financial centers that we would expect.

TABLE 6.5

INTEGRATION BENCHMARKS FOR JAMES' SERIES, 1888 TO 1911

						DW	R^2	rho
Interurban								
ln bos	=	.141	+	.741	ln nyc	1.55	.497	---
		(.152)		(.110)				
ln chi	=	1.27	+	.106	ln nyc	2.33	.432	.604
		(.188)		(.127)				(.117)
ln sfo	=	1.51	−	.021	ln nyc	2.18	.759	.898
		(.328)		(.097)				(.075)
ln sfo	=	1.43	+	.040	ln chi	2.20	.760	.896
		(.331)		(.120)				(.076)
Regional								
ln ny	=	1.25	+	.087	ln nyc	2.19	.355	.575
		(.118)		(.080)				(.121)
ln il	=	1.54	+	.026	ln chi	2.50	.708	.816
		(.108)		(.060)				(.082)
ln mo	=	1.40	+	.304	ln stl	2.00	.342	---
		(.094)		(.060)				

NOTES: All regressions in Tables 6.5 through 6.14 were estimated by the Ordinary Least Squares method; where a value is given for rho, the regression was estimated using the Cochrane–Orcutt technique to correct for serial correlation. Standard errors are given in parantheses.

All variables are logarithmic transformations of James' [1974] semi–annual bank earning rate series for 1888 to 1911.

A benchmark of the relationship between more distant financial centers is captured in the regression relating the Chicago rate to the New York City rate. Here, the interest differential is much higher, at 1.27, and the sensitivity is much lower at 0.106. At greatest distance are the San Francisco and New York City financial centers. The regressions suggest little relationship between national bank earning rates in San Francisco and those in New York City. There is a large measured interest differential (a = 1.51) and no significant statistical relationship between the two rates. These results are consistent with the historical evidence suggesting that San Francisco was isolated from (or, at least, not well connected to) the financial giant of the eastern United States.

In addition to measuring the relationship between financial centers, we need to create benchmarks for the relationship between hinterlands and their nearest financial center in order to gauge the status of the regional (as opposed to interurban) market. Consequently, both an eastern (New York state-New York City) and a midwestern (Illinois-Chicago) regional benchmark are presented. Surprisingly, the relationship between these states and their centers is not as close as expected from the descriptive literature. There are large interest differentials between city and hinterland, and the sensitivity coefficient is small and not statistically different from zero. It appears that the size and proximity of the financial center does not guarantee a close correlation with hinterland banks. Perhaps a better benchmark of regional integration is given by the Missouri-St. Louis regression. Here, the sensitivity coefficient is a more reasonable 0.304.

Simple Regional Results

In Table 6.6, both California and Washington show a strong (in benchmark terms) and statistically significant relationship to San Francisco, which is as we would expect, given San Francisco's geographical centrality in California, and the status of Washington as a financial outpost of San Francisco. The smaller sensitivity coefficient for California compared to that for Washington may reflect the rather strong distinction between Southern California and Northern California. Southern California was less dominated by San Francisco, since the section had great local wealth and a growing financial center in Los Angeles. Washington, on the other hand, had lower levels of

TABLE 6.6

PACIFIC COAST INTEGRATION

							DW	R^2	rho
To San Francisco									
ln ca	=	1.45	+	.285	ln sfo		1.86	.342	---
		(.098)		(.058)					
ln or	=	1.88	−	.016	ln sfo		1.43	.000	---
		(.226)		(.134)					
ln wa	=	1.48	+	.374	ln sfo		1.68	.178	---
		(.200)		(.118)					
To NewYork City									
ln ca	=	1.87	+	.035	ln nyc		2.12	.166	.409
		(.141)		(.100)					(.139)
ln or	=	1.62	+	.172	ln nyc		1.56	.020	---
		(.247)		(.178)					
ln wa	=	2.04	+	.038	ln nyc		2.08	.096	.307
		(.261)		(.187)					(.141)
To Chicago									
ln ca	=	1.61	+	.218	ln chi		1.49	.119	---
		(.127)		(.087)					
ln or	=	1.72	+	.099	ln chi		1.48	.007	---
		(.251)		(.172)					
ln wa	=	1.39	+	.498	ln chi		1.71	.187	---
		(.223)		(.143)					

indigenous savings and was compelled to seek funds from San Francisco. Neither state shows a significant relationship to New York City, but both evince clear connection to Chicago. This is probably due to the impact of Chicago when railroad connections to the East were opened, as mentioned previously.

The results for Oregon are a bit puzzling. There is a large interest differential, and no statistically significant relationship between Oregon rates and San Francisco rates. It is clear from the historical literature that Oregon, as the older and more slowly growing state, had fewer demands made on its available savings supply than did Washington, and so turned to outside financial markets less frequently.

Reserve City Dummies

A more obvious problem causing difficulty in interpreting the Oregon results is the discontinuity in the data series occurring in 1899 when Portland was granted reserve city status. At this point, all banks in Portland were removed from the country bank figures making up the state rate, and were aggregated to form a Portland reserve city rate.[58] A regression of Oregon on San Francisco which includes a dummy variable for the period after the removal of Portland banks is presented in Table 6.7. As can be seen, the switch of Portland banks from country to reserve city status has a very large and statistically significant effect. The dummy coefficient indicates that the constant term, representing the ratio or differential of Oregon country bank rates to San Francisco rates, is 0.448 larger when Portland banks are excluded from country banks. This suggests that Portland banks were very different from the rest of the banks in Oregon. Perhaps hinterland banks were not well-connected to the city or transactions costs or risk premiums were much higher for country banks.[59] The effect of correcting for this discontinuity in the data series is dramatic: now, in the regression equation with San Francisco there is a large and significant b coefficient, implying a close link between San Francisco and hinterland bank rates in Oregon.

Both the California and the Washington series are also affected by the data redefinition. In 1900, Los Angeles became a reserve city; and in Washington, Seattle in 1906 and Spokane and Tacoma in 1908 joined the ranks of reserve cities. In California, however, there is no significant reserve dummy effect as was seen in

TABLE 6.7

RESERVE CITY DUMMIES

					DW	R^2	rho
Los Angeles exits, 1900							
ln ca	= 1.63	+ .198	ln sfo –	.076 CADUM	1.88	.355	---
	(.206)	(.106)		(.078)			
Portland exits, 1899							
ln or	= .835	+ .484	ln sfo +	.448 ORDUM	1.55	.145	---
	(.436)	(.221)		(.162)			
Seattle exits, 1906							
ln wa	= 1.35	+ .440	ln sfo +	.104 WADUM1	1.70	.189	---
	(.261)	(.146)		(.132)			
Spokane and Tacoma exit, 1908							
ln wa	= 1.37	+ .425	ln sfo +	.214 WADUM2	1.71	.221	---
	(.209)	(.121)		(.135)			

NOTES: Reserve dummies are lagged one period from actual date of city exit to account for James' method of lagging loan and discount values one period when calculating interest rates. His method incorrectly results in a one period drop in the state rate, since gross earnings which exclude the new reserve city's earnings in period t are divided by loans and discounts of period t–1 which include those of the new city.

CADUM = 0 for 1888:1 to 1900:2; = 1 for 1901:1 to 1911:2
ORDUM = 0 for 1888:1 to 1899:2; = 1 for 1900:1 to 1911:2
WADUM1 = 0 for 1888:1 to 1906:2; = 1 for 1907:1 to 1911:2
WADUM2 = 0 for 1888:1 to 1908:2 ; = 1 for 1909:1 to 1911:2

the case of Oregon. This suggests that the behavior or characteristics of country banks in California was not significantly different from the behavior of reserve city banks in the state. This may be interpreted as resulting from the integrated market tying together banks in the cities and the outlying areas of California. The exit of Seattle in 1906 also had little effect on the regression results. The dummy coefficient is negative, suggesting that Seattle rates may actually have been slightly higher than other banks, which included the banks in the cities of Spokane and Tacoma before 1908. The dummy for the exit of Spokane and Tacoma in 1908 has the expected positive sign, but it is small and not statistically different from zero. Again, these results suggest the existence of some network within Washington which prevented large differences between country and city banks.[60]

Convergence of Interest Rates

These econometric results suggest that the states of the Pacific Coast formed a regional banking market at least as "integrated" over the period as some regional markets in the East and the Midwest. If there is a connection to an outside center for this region, it may be to Chicago and not to New York City. There is a positive sensitivity of San Francisco rates to Chicago rates, and a smaller interest differential between San Francisco and Chicago than between San Francisco and New York. The historical precedents for a San Francisco-Chicago relationship exist, since Chicago merchants were said to have flooded into San Francisco with the opening of the transcontinental railroad.

Since most authors test the changing level of integration over the period by measuring the decline of interest differentials, it might be instructive to construct similar tests for the Pacific Coast region. To do so, a time trend variable is added to the independent regressors. A negative coefficient on this variable would indicate that the constant term a (measuring the ratio of the rates, or the interest differential) was declining over time: the dependent rate was converging upon the independent rate. This technique allows a measure of convergence at the same time that each rate is experiencing common non-trend fluctuations. Thus, we can examine both the convergence form and the covariability form of integration.

Table 6.8 presents results which capture the movement of the interest differential as measured by the coefficient on the natural

TABLE 6.8
INTEREST RATE CONVERGENCE

											DW	R^2	rho
	ln bos	=	.192	+	.730	ln nyc	–	.012	ln time		1.53	.498	---
			(.215)		(.116)			(.036)					
	ln chi	=	1.40	+	.367	ln nyc	–	.159	ln time		1.51	.465	---
			(.219)		(.118)			(.037)					
	ln ny	=	1.72	+	.061	ln nyc	–	.142	ln time		2.08	.464	---
			(.173)		(.075)			(.040)					
	ln il	=	2.04	+	.065	ln chi	–	.176	ln time		2.12	.790	.320
			(.141)		(.056)			(.027)					(.131)
	ln sfo	=	3.52	–	.037	ln nyc	–	.588	ln time		2.18	.804	.672
			(.491)		(.097)			(.146)					(.081)
	ln sfo	=	3.43	+	.027	ln chi	–	.588	ln time		2.20	.803	.678
			(.583)		(.118)			(.163)					(.080)
	ln ca	=	1.93	+	.145	ln sfo	–	.084	ln time		2.09	.427	---
			(.205)		(.077)			(.032)					
*	ln or	=	1.72	+	.318	ln sfo	–	.248	ln time		1.99	.326	---
			(.469)		(.204)			(.072)					
	ln wa	=	2.02	+	.217	ln sfo	–	.094	ln time		1.73	.210	---
			(.197)		(.092)			(.030)					
	ln ca	=	2.40	–	.069	ln nyc	–	.132	ln time		2.02	.392	---
			(.469)		(.204)			(.072)					
*	ln or	=	2.62	–	.118	ln nyc	–	.298	ln time		1.92	.296	---
			(.357)		(.172)			(.134)					
	ln wa	=	2.72	–	.097	ln nyc	–	.166	ln time		1.71	.186	---
			(.311)		(.168)			(.052)					
	ln ca	=	2.33	–	.020	ln chi	–	.130	ln time		1.95	.383	---
			(.197)		(.092)			(.030)					
*	ln or	=	2.36	+	.022	ln chi	–	.270	ln time		1.96	.289	---
			(.404)		(.186)			(.079)					
	ln wa	=	1.92	+	.322	ln chi	–	.096	ln time		1.76	.231	---
			(.400)		(.186)			(.060)					

*estimated using ORDUM as a regressor

logarithm of time. Again, as a benchmark, the Boston-New York City differential shows little decrease over the period, suggesting that a well-integrated market predated 1888. Chicago, however, was still "integrating" to New York City over the period, since the coefficient on the time variable is -0.159, which is statistically significant.[61] While San Francisco's non-trend sensitivity to New York City and Chicago is still unclear, the very large coefficient on the logarithm of time is evidence that San Francisco rates were declining rapidly toward eastern and midwestern levels throughout the period. This, in earlier authors' terms, is a picture of San Francisco "integrating" to the rest of the national market. The lack of sensitivity to the New York rate suggests, however, that integration was not evident in a fine level of coordination. The convergence could be due to declining costs or risks in San Francisco relative to the New York market.

The regression results for the Pacific Coast states reinforce the notion that San Francisco's hinterland was sensitive to the city's rates, and that outlying areas were converging to the San Francisco level. The most rapid convergence occurred with Oregon rates; this is understandable given the larger size of the Oregon-San Francisco differential. Thus, while the sensitivity measure *b* reflects the existence of a market connection to San Francisco, the declining interest differentials captured in the coefficient on the time variable indicate that funds were flowing through these channels to reduce excess demand in outlying rates, or that improving connections were reducing transactions costs or risk premiums attached to outlying investments.[62]

Lags in Interest Rate Response

Another indication of the degree of integration may be seen in an analysis which includes lagged values of the independent variable. The speed with which changes in city rates are translated into changes in hinterland rates reflects the efficiency of the market in transmitting local shocks or information. Thus, while a market may fully reflect changes in one rate over the long run, the speed with which this market reacts is also important. Table 6.9 presents estimates of the speed of adjustment to current and lagged values of rates in financial centers.

With the possibility of lagged effects, San Francisco still shows little relationship to the New York City rate. Eastern rates of one year earlier do not affect the current San Francisco rate. On the other hand,

TABLE 6.9

REGRESSIONS WITH LAGGED INTEREST RATES

	ln sfo	= 1.59	− .030 ln nyc_t	− .012 ln nyc_{t-1}	− .050 ln nyc_{t-2}
		(.472)	(.112)	(.118)	(.112)
sum	ln nyc	= −.090;	DW = 2.20;	R^2 = .756;	rho = .892
		(.260)			(.079)
	ln sfo	= 1.37	+ .025 ln chi_t	− .029 ln chi_{t-1}	+ .081 ln chi_{t-2}
		(.558)	(.141)	(.162)	(.168)
sum	ln chi	= .077;	DW = 2.21;	R^2 = .757;	rho = .885
		(.343)			(.082)
	ln ca	= 1.39	+ .076 ln sfo_t	+ .074 ln sfo_{t-1}	+ .167 ln sfo_{t-2}
		(.103)	(.121)	(.153)	(.139)
sum	ln sfo	= .317;	DW = 1.85;	R^2 = .394	
		(.061)			
*	ln or	= .597	+ .415 ln sfo_t	+ .124 ln sfo_{t-1}	+ .045 ln sfo_{t-2}
		(.518)	(.277)	(.343)	(.311)
sum	ln sfo	= .585;	DW = 1.69;	R^2 = .194	
		(.261)			
	ln wa	= 1.42	+ .147 ln sfo_t	− .108 ln sfo_{t-1}	+ .304 ln sfo_{t-2}
		(.218)	(.255)	(.323)	(.294)
sum	ln sfo	= .404;	DW = 1.66;	R^2 = .200	
		(.129)			
	ln ca	= 1.90	+ .009 ln nyc_t	− .077 ln nyc_{t-1}	+ .069 ln nyc_{t-2}
		(.232)	(.100)	(.100)	(.100)
sum	ln nyc	= .001;	DW = 2.23 ;	R^2 = .169;	rho = .379
		(.170)			(.144)

TABLE 6.9

(continued)

*	ln or	= 1.55	+ .076	$\ln nyc_t$	+ .076	$\ln nyc_{t-1}$	− .008	$\ln nyc_{t-2}$
		(.332)	(.200)		(.213)		(.200)	
sum	ln nyc	= .144;		DW = 1.63;		R^2 = .093		
		(.238)						
	ln wa	= 2.04	+ .024	$\ln nyc_t$	− .123	$\ln nyc_{t-1}$	+ .130	$\ln nyc_{t-2}$
		(.328)	(.202)		(.215)		(.200)	
sum	ln nyc	= .031;		DW = 1.42;		R^2 = .013		
		(.240)						
	ln ca	= 1.46	+ .016	$\ln chi_t$	− .122	$\ln chi_{t-1}$	+ .430	$\ln chi_{t-2}$
		(.135)	(.113)		(.119)		(.126)	
sum	ln chi	= .324;		DW = 1.66;		R^2 = .301		
		(.094)						
*	ln or	= .919	− .025	$\ln chi_t$	+ .273	$\ln chi_{t-1}$	+ .270	$\ln chi_{t-2}$
		(.415)	(.233)		(.246)		(.308)	
sum	ln chi	= .519;		DW = 1.71;		R^2 = .177		
		(.257)						
	ln wa	= 1.37	+ 4.16	$\ln chi_t$	− .152	$\ln chi_{t-1}$	+ .246	$\ln chi_{t-2}$
		(.269)	(.226)		(.238)		(.252)	
sum	ln chi	= .510;		DW = 1.72;		R^2 = .180		
		(.188)						

NOTES: * = estimated using ORDUM as a regressor
sum = sum of variable coefficients over time

while Chicago's rate of one year previous shows a small positive relationship to the San Francisco rates, it is not statistically different from zero. California's hinterland shows a positive and significant relationship to San Francisco, with the greatest sensitivity to the one year lagged rate. Little correspondence with New York City is seen, but California rates exhibit a large sensitivity to Chicago rates of one year previous. Oregon appears to have been quick to respond to changes in the San Francisco rate, since more than two-thirds of the Oregon response comes in the first period. Oregon rates show little responsiveness to the New York City rate, but are sensitive to the Chicago rate after a lag of one period. As with California, Washington's greatest sensitivity to San Francisco rate changes comes after a one year lag, although Washington had a larger current response and a larger long run response to San Francisco than California did. As with all other states, little or no overall sensitivity to New York City is seen in Washington. The most interesting result is that Washington appears to be highly sensitive to the current rate in Chicago. This may result from Washington's close connections to Chicago via the railroads and the wheat markets.

Financial Markets in the 1890s

Many authors, Kindleberger in particular, have seen the true test of a financial market occurring in times of stress, especially during financial panics and economic depressions.[63] The period under study here includes an interval of panic and depression--the Great Depression of the 1890s, which commenced with the Panic of 1893 and continued until 1896 or 1897 before recovery started.[64] This provides another type of test of market integration--a test of how well markets performed under stress.

The Pacific Coast region was not immune to this nationwide depression, as it had been in earlier periods.[65] California's wheat industry collapsed in the 1890s, compounding the general economic crisis of the period.[66] Tattersall claims that "the slumps of 1893, 1896 . . . appear to have been more severe in the Northwest than nationally,"[67] with the impact on Washington being more severe but not as prolonged as the impact on Oregon. A hint of the magnitude of the agricultural crisis in the Pacific Northwest can be seen in Table 6.10 which shows little increase in wheat production from 1893 to 1896

TABLE 6.10

WHEAT PRODUCTION IN THE PACIFIC NORTHWEST
1892–1899

	Acreage Harvested (000)	Production (bushels, millions)	Oregon Price (bu)	Washington Price (bu)	Wholesale PriceIndex (1926=100)
1892	1225	22.1	$ .64	$ .58	52
1893	1350	26.8	.55	.48	53
1894	1425	26.3	.43	.39	48
1895	1460	25.9	.47	.41	49
1896	1570	27.3	.72	.74	47
1897	1800	35.9	.72	.68	47
1898	2065	41.2	.62	.54	49
1899	2101	38.9	.53	.51	52

NOTES: Data from James Tattersall, "The Economic Development of the Pacific Northwest to 1920" (Ph.D. diss., University of Washington, 1960), 163–165.

while the price of wheat in Oregon fell from $.64 per bushel in 1892 to $.47 in 1895. In the same period, the price fell from $.58 to $.41 in Washington. Agricultural and economic stress were reflected in the banking sector as well. Between 1893 and 1898, the number of national banks in Oregon fell from 39 to 29; in the same period, the number fell from 64 to 33 in Washington while there was no net change in the number of national banks in California. In October 1896, one of the low points of the depression, 21 percent of Oregon national bank were in liquidation (56 percent for insolvency); 48 percent of Washington national banks were in liquidation (54 percent for insolvency); and 35 percent of California national banks were in liquidation (29 percent for insolvency). The magnitude of the depression can also be seen in reference to Figure 6.8 which shows the trend of loans and discounts made by national banks between 1892 and 1898. It is clear that San Francisco and California suffered the least disruption in loan activity relative to Washington and Oregon, which might be expected, given their more diversified economic base. The Pacific Northwest, where activity was highly concentrated in agricultural and extractive industry, suffered the most. James' interest rate proxy also reflects the disruption occurring in the financial markets during this period, with low rates prevailing during the depressed periods, and a jump in rates occurring during the financial uncertainty surrounding the silver question in the 1896 McKinley-Bryan presidential campaign.

If a regional market were in place on the Coast, we would expect to see San Francisco acting as a lender of last resort during the crisis periods of 1893 and 1896.[68] Thus, there should be a flow of bankers' balances from San Francisco to the hinterland, and we might expect interest differentials to decline as rates on loans in the center increase as a result. David Baerncopf hypothesizes that interest differentials would increase during depressions as funds are withdrawn from the hinterland and deposited in the "safe haven" of the financial center.[69] This would have the effect of raising hinterland rates and reducing center rates. The net effect on hinterland interest rates during depressions is not clear, however, since rates tend to be very low in depressed periods due to a lack of economic activity and deflation.

The trends in bankers' balances clearly reflect the effect of panic and depression on San Francisco and the Pacific Coast region. Table 6.11 presents data on the ratio of bankers' balances to individual deposits in national banks at the fifth call (September or October). This ratio represents the proportion of a bank's liabilities (deposits) that is

TABLE 6.11

RATIOS OF BANKERS' BALANCES TO DEPOSITS, 1892–1899

Due from Reserve Agents/Individual Deposits

At national banks in:	SFO	CA	OR	WA
Sept 1892	.062	.125	.096	.141
Oct 1893	.022	.051	.043	.045
Oct 1894	.047	.138	.167	.098
Sept 1895	.115	.128	.136	.113
Oct 1896	.090	.081	.082	.082
Oct 1897	.035	.131	.154	.173
Sept 1898	.051	.158	.153	.242
Sept 1899	.062	.183	.280	.286

Due from Other Banks/Individual Deposits

At national banks in:	SFO	CA	OR	WA
Sept 1892	.160	.090	.150	.129
Oct 1893	.125	.095	.090	.105
Oct 1894	.060	.062	.134	.114
Sept 1895	.079	.075	.106	.136
Oct 1896	.095	.068	.097	.142
Oct 1897	.082	.070	.227	.252
Sept 1898	.192	.085	.112	.176
Sept 1899	.317	.118	.114	.125

Due to Other Banks/Individual Deposits

At national banks in:	SFO
Sept 1892	.366
Oct 1893	.198
Oct 1894	.324
Sept 1895	.353
Oct 1896	.265
Oct 1897	.315
Sept 1898	.317
Sept 1899	.450

NOTES: From *Annual Reports* of U.S. Comptroller of the Currency, 1892–1899.

kept in a very safe, liquid form. The ratio drops sharply in 1893 and 1896 for the Pacific Coast states as they withdrew funds from correspondents and reserve agents; the ratio rises above pre-panic levels during the depressed periods as funds were placed in safe, liquid, interest-bearing form. Note also the ratio of "Due to Banks" for San Francisco. This drops during the panics as the city provided funds, and rises during the depression as funds were deposited in San Francisco.

Dummy variables were created for both panic periods (1893 and 1896) and for the depression period (1894-1895); both were added as regressors to test the effect of such periods on interest differentials. These regressions are presented in Table 6.12. There appears to be no statistically significant change in the interest differential between San Francisco and New York City or between San Francisco and most of its hinterland in this period.[70] In general, interest differentials were smaller on average during panics (the coefficient on the panic dummy is less than zero), and larger during depressions (the coefficient on the depression dummy is greater than zero) for the San Francisco-New York, California-San Francisco, and Oregon-San Francisco regressions. On the other hand, the Washington-San Francisco differential declines throughout the 1890s. Only the panic dummies for California and Oregon and the depression dummy for Washington are statistically different from zero. If 1896 alone is employed as the "panic" period, we find that interest differentials were lower in panics (because of a rise in city rates as funds were withdrawn to the hinterland in liquidity crises) to a significant degree in Oregon and California. The events of 1893 do not seem to have had the same impact on the West as the East; there is a clear jump in rates in 1893:2 (March to September 1893) in New York City and Chicago, but not in the Pacific Coast region.

The pattern of interest differentials between hinterland and center during the unstable years of 1893 to 1897 is clearly difficult to analyze. A more general test of the relationship between city and hinterland rates is given in Table 6.13, where regressions employing an interactive dummy variable are presented. This variable attempts to capture changes in the sensitivity (*b*) of outlying rates to the San Francisco rate. During times of financial stress, there may be some reduction in the efficiency of the market mechanism to coordinate movements in interest rates through capital flows.[71] "Thinner" hinterland markets, especially, would be characterized by higher interest volatility in the face of shocks to the demand or supply of funds. Although the

TABLE 6.12

PANIC AND DEPRESSION DUMMIES

				DW	R^2	rho
ln sfo	= 1.51	− .021 ln nyc	+ .001 PANDUM	2.18	.759	.898
	(.333)	(.101)	(.101)			(.101)
ln sfo	= 1.50	− .012 ln nyc	+ .064 DEPDUM	2.17	.760	.895
	(.324)	(.100)	(.142)			(.077)
ln ca	= 1.41	+ .314 ln sfo	− .145 PANDUM	1.97	.388	---
	(.098)	(.059)	(.078)			
* ln or	= .866	+ .500 ln sfo	− .365 PANDUM	1.65	.228	---
	(.419)	(.212)	(.168)			
ln wa	= 1.43	+ .417 ln sfo	− .213 PANDUM	1.75	.208	---
	(.203)	(.122)	(.163)			
ln ca	= 1.47	+ .269 ln sfo	+ .072 DEPDUM	1.85	.353	---
	(.101)	(.061)	(.081)			
* ln or	= .839	+ .465 ln sfo	+ .204 DEPDUM	1.48	.170	---
	(.434)	(.220)	(.174)			
ln wa	= 1.40	+ .443 ln sfo	− .318 DEPDUM	1.88	.244	---
	(.199)	(.120)	(.160)			

*estimated using ORDUM as a regressor

NOTES: PANDUM = dummy variable for periods of financial panic
= 0 for 1888:1–1893:1, 1895:1–1896:1, 1897:2–1911:2
= 1 for 1893:2–1894:1, 1896:2–1897:1

DEPDUM = dummy variable for periods of economic depression
= 0 for 1888:1–1894:1, 1896:2–1911:2
= 1 for 1894:2–1896:1

TABLE 6.13

INTERACTIVE DUMMY FOR PERIODS OF FINANCIAL STRESS

									DW	R^2	rho
ln sfo	=	1.53	−	.036 ln nyc	+	.094	DUMNYC		2.16	.764	.883
		(.290)		(.100)		(.106)					(.081)
ln sfo	=	1.42	+	.039 ln chi	+	.101	DUMCHI		2.17	.766	.877
		(.290)		(.121)		(.094)					(.084)
ln ca	=	1.42	+	.313 ln sfo	−	.030	DUMSFO		1.87	.357	---
		(.111)		(.069)		(.030)					
* ln or	=	.810	+	.538 ln sfo	−	.098	DUMSFO		1.63	.188	---
		(.448)		(.228)		(.066)					
ln wa	=	1.22	+	.574 ln sfo	−	.167	DUMSFO		1.96	.319	---
		(.209)		(.129)		(.057)					

---

* estimated using ORDUM as a regressor

NOTES: DUM = dummy variable for economic stress of 1890s
DUMNYC = DUM*ln nyc
DUMCHI = DUM*ln chi
DUMSFO = DUM*ln sfo

where DUM = 0 for 1888:1–1892:2, 1898:1–1911:2
= 1 for 1893:1–1897:2

results in Table 6.13 are lacking in statistical significance for the most part, the interactive dummy DUMSFO suggests that there was a decoupling of rates in the regional market in the depression period. The covariability of California and San Francisco rates was reduced only slightly, the covariability of Oregon and San Francisco rates decreased a small amount more, while the coordination of rate movements between Washington and San Francisco was decreased considerably. This accords with Tattersall's impression that Washington was hit by more severe shocks than Oregon, and with the impression that California probably weathered the crisis better than the Pacific Northwest. The Pacific Coast regional market, thus, was not developed enough to smooth out crises completely. There was some breakdown in the financial network, especially between the San Francisco and the states of the Pacific Northwest.

Caveats

This chapter has presented a number of very simple econometric tests for regional market integration using the standard data set available to economic historians who analyze financial development in the period prior to the organization of the Federal Reserve System. At a general level, the notion of a market, centered on San Francisco, and serving the financial needs of California, Oregon, and Washington is borne out in the national bank interest rate data. Furthermore, isolation from New York City did *not* imply a lack of financial market development in the region as previous works seem to suggest. The Pacific Northwest states were more dependent upon the San Francisco funds market than was the state of California which could draw upon the financial capital of Los Angeles as well. The connection of the Pacific Coast states was closer to San Francisco than to New York City; the relevant financial center outside the region was Chicago rather than New York City.

The acceptance of these conclusions must be tempered by the recognition that the regression results are only as reliable as the data used. First, it must be remembered that we are looking at national bank behavior, and so cannot make definite conclusions about the full regional market, except insofar as national banks had behavior similar to other types of financial institutions on the Coast. James' technical approach to creating a proxy for the interest rate on loans and discounts does not appear to have any major flaws; in fact, Smiley suggests a similar approach in his dissertation although he uses a simpler earning rate for private assets in his analysis and published work.

The underlying data from the Comptroller reports, on the other hand, are of uncertain quality.[72] It is surprising that few authors other than Smiley have pointed out the possible difficulties in constructing interest rate proxies using the published national bank data. The individual and aggregated bank balance sheet data are relatively consistent from year to year, but the gross earnings figures, which are key in the construction of interest rate proxies, have rather large fluctuations, especially in the turbulent 1890s. Smiley suggests it is unlikely that these swings were due solely to changes in earnings resulting from interest rates fluctuations on loans and discounts. He feels that there were three alternative causes of such fluctuations. First, bank liquidations in which all assets were sold off, possibly at below book value, would be counted as an increase in gross earnings and losses. Second, bank mergers may have resulted in the sale of excess physical plant, also counted as gross earnings. Finally, there is the possibility of Comptroller tabulation error.[73]

Since it is very difficult in practice to distinguish between these irregularities, Smiley undertakes a smoothing of the occasional wide swings in the data, based upon the trends in accounts of nearby states or cities.[74] It is not clear that such smoothing techniques are appropriate, but Smiley apparently feels that they are of less harm than the discontinuities in the data series. Accordingly, he adjusts the figures for 21 states and reserve cities in a small number of periods. For the Pacific Coast region, he adjusts only California's very low gross earnings of July 1907 to June 1908. (Gross earnings in these two periods were approximately 75 percent below earnings in the surrounding periods.) Smiley is not certain of the cause of the radical drop in earnings, but he uses Oregon and Washington trends to adjust the figures upward.[75] Apparently, Smiley did not notice the swings in earnings for Oregon and Washington during the 1890s, and James overlooked (intentionally or not) all swings. James does mention, in a footnote, the earnings fluctuations for Lincoln, Nebraska in the 1890s.[76] He suggests that the swings might be due to the fact that interest on discounts accrues, but is not received, until the maturity date. Thus, while the loan may be on the books throughout one or more earnings periods, the earnings will not actually be received until the end period, resulting in a sharp swing in earnings without a change in the interest charged on the discount.

The question faced in research using national bank data is the extent to which the data should be smoothed, perhaps incorrectly, with the loss of the measures of interest sensitivity sought by using James' semi-annual series. On the other hand, to what extent should the data remain unsmoothed, thus risking the loss of statistical (or even economic) significance? Some in-year fluctuations may result from agricultural seasonality, or the possibility that discounted loans which were on the books in two periods paid interest only in the second period. The seasonality question is examined in Table 6.14, where a dummy for the harvest period (the first earnings period of the reporting year) is added as a regressor. The dummy shows some small positive effect on interest differentials, implying that rates were somewhat higher during the harvest season when demand for funds to move crops was high.

The most radical fluctuations in gross earnings--and so in the interest rate proxy--occurred during times of financial stress, especially the depression of the 1890s. (See Figures 6.9a-6.9d for graphs of the movements in earnings in the Pacific region.) This is unfortunate insofar as it makes difficult fine tests of interest rate behavior during the crisis, as was seen in the previous section. On the other hand, the large fluctuations are telling insofar as they reflect disruptions in banking activity resulting from rapid liquidations of bank assets or bank failures. It is highly unlikely that the clustering of these swings in the 1890s was due to Comptroller accountants being differentially inept during that period. The pattern of swings most prominent in Oregon and Washington (California has only one strong swing in 1897-1898, and the San Francisco series is relatively smooth throughout the 1890s) is one of high gross earnings and losses one period followed by low earnings and losses the next.

For example, in Oregon gross earnings rose from $362,118 to $617,220 between 1895:1 and 1896:1 while the sum of losses and premiums rose from $108,521 to $405,161 even though the number of banks remained constant. This is consistent with banks selling large amounts of assets at a loss, presumably in search of liquidity.[77] Earnings and losses plus premiums then fell dramatically to $292,893 and $53,293, respectively, in 1896:1 as the number of operating banks fell from 35 to 32, even though total loans outstanding declined only one million dollars.

TABLE 6.14

SEASONAL VARIATION IN INTEREST RATES

				DW	R^2	rho
ln sfo	= 1.44	− .007 ln nyc	+ .063 SEASDUM	2.07	.786	.911
	(.356)	(.092)	(.027)			(.072)
ln sfo	= 1.40	+ .033 ln chi	+ .063 SEASDUM	2.09	.786	.909
	(.356)	(.114)	(.027)			(.073)
ln ca	= 1.43	+ .275 ln sfo	+ .064 SEASDUM	1.73	.374	---
	(.098)	(.058)	(.042)			
* ln or	= .902	+ .407 ln sfo	+ .167 SEASDUM	1.36	.205	---
	(.427)	(.219)	(.160)			
ln wa	= 1.48	+ .369 ln sfo	+ .033 SEASDUM	1.67	.180	---
	(.204)	(.120)	(.089)			

* estimated using ORDUM as a regressor

NOTES: SEASDUM = dummy variable for seasonal swings in rates
= 1 for period 1 interest rate (which includes harvest period)
= 0 for period 2

In Washington, sharp swings in the late 1890s result from similar fluctuations in gross earnings which, by looking at corresponding movements in losses, suggest the sale of assets at a loss (or some very creative accounting practice which postponed the charge-off of losses until large earnings were amassed). For example, earnings rose from $469,739 in 1899:1 to $892,938 in 1899:2, while losses and premiums rose from $78,044 to $586,680 even though the number of banks declined. This could be the result of bank mergers between national banks and the sale of excess physical plant, or the result of the liquidation of two national banks with the Comptroller accounting for the sale of all assets as gross earnings. Why this occurs in 1899 is not clear.[78]

It is interesting to note the lack of similar radical swings in the 1890s in California or San Francisco (excepting the swing in California in 1898). Were accounting methods in California different? Or is the stability of banking in that area captured by the interest rate proxies? The number of national banks in California in the period from 1892 to 1899 fluctuated only between 29 and 36 , while the number of national banks in San Francisco was constant through 1898. In the same period, the number of Oregon national banks ranged from 29 to 41, while in Washington the number fluctuated between 30 and 70. These wide swings in numbers of banks are clearly a large part of the explanation for volatility in the interest rate proxies in the 1890s. The number of national banks on the Pacific Coast grew steadily throughout the rest of the period, and the interest rate series shows no further swings of the magnitude of those in the 1890s.

CONCLUSIONS

The Pacific Coast region did form a financial network centered on San Francisco. The medium-term earning rates of national banks exhibit a sensitivity to the San Francisco rate of equal or greater value than benchmark coefficients created for city-city and city-hinterland relationships in the more developed parts of the United States.[79] Short-term funds flows in the region were coordinated throughout the year, and long-term mortgage interest rates display a high degree of correlation. While enough market segmentation existed to preclude complete and instantaneous interest rate arbitrage across the region, the market was able to mobilize funds throughout the states of the Pacific Coast. The region's isolation from the New York financial center *did not*, as some economic historians seem to imply, result in financial backwardness.

NOTES

1. See Penelope Hartland, "Interregional Payments Compared with International Payments," *Quarterly Journal of Economics* 63 (August, 1949); Paul Simpson, *Regional Aspects of Business Cycles and Special Studies of the Pacific Northwest* (Study prepared for the Bonneville Administration, Eugene, Oregon, 1953); Werner Hochwald, "Conceptual Issues of Regional Income Estimation," in Conference on Research in Income and Wealth *Regional Income* (Princeton: Princeton University Press, 1957); Robert Allen and Donald Watson, *The Structure of the Oregon Economy: An Input/Output Study* (Eugene, Oregon: Bureau of Business and Economic Research, University of Oregon, 1965); and Phillip Bourque et al., *The Washington Economy: An Input-Output Study* (Seattle: University of Washington Graduate School of Business Administration, 1967) for work with contemporary data. For historical use of these techniques, see Tattersall, "Economic Development of the Pacific Northwest;" Albert Fishlow, "Antebellum Interregional Trade Reconsidered," *American Economic Review* 54 (May 1964); and John James, *Money and Capital Markets.*
2. This sort of distinction was used by federal authorities when the Federal Intermediate Credit Banks and Federal Land Banks were established in the 1920s.
3. For example, the Preferred Habitats hypothesis of Franco Modigliani and Richard Sutch ["Innovations in Interest Rate Policy," *American Economic Review* 56 (May 1966) and "Debt Management and the Term Structure of Interest Rates: An Empirical Analysis of Recent Experience," *Journal of Political Economy* 85 (Supplement, August 1967)] places emphasis on relative supplies and demands for funds at each maturity in determining yield.
4. Sushka and Barrett, "Banking Structure and the National Capital Market" is one exception, but neither their data nor their methodology are particularly rigorous.
5. This was a continuation of the work of Edwin Kemmerer, *Seasonal Variations in the Relative Demand for Money and*

Capital in the United States (Washington, D.C.: Government Printing Office, 1910).

6. See John James [*Money and Capital Markets*, 127-137] for an excellent discussion of seasonal variations and the correspondent banking system.
7. Allyn Young ["An Analysis of Bank Statistics for the United States," *Review of Economic Statistics* Part I: 6 (October 1924); Part II: 7 (January 1925); Part III: 7 (April 1925)] uses the Comptroller's definition of the Pacific region: California, Oregon, Washington, Idaho, Utah, Nevada, and Arizona.
8. This is as opposed to New York City or Chicago, whose activities are more national in scope. See Allyn Young "Analysis of Bank Statistics" (April 1925), 91.
9. See Albert Greef, *The Commercial Paper House in the United States* (New York: Arno Press, 1975) for an excellent history of the development of the commercial paper market.
10. Greef, *The Commercial Paper House*, 39.
11. Davis, "The Investment Market," 372-373. Greef claims that commercial paper houses would be unnecessary if banks had been able to establish branches nationwide. Greef, *The Commercial Paper House*, 412.
12. Greef, *The Commercial Paper House*, 203.
13. Breckenridge in "Discount Rates," uses Bradstreet's quotations in his analysis of barriers to capital mobility in the United States.
14. It is interesting, and telling, that Pacific Coast rates were not more carefully quoted. This may be evidence of a lack of interest by Easterners in Pacific region commercial paper.
15. U.S. Bureau of the Census, *Report on Real Estate Mortgages at the Eleventh Census* (Washington, D.C.: Government Printing Office, 1895), 246.
16. See Eichengreen, "Mortgage Rates in the Populist Era," 1012-1013.
17. Kenneth Snowden, "Mortgage Rates," 676-682, seems to argue for this view.
18. I avoid using the New York City-New York state relationship because a large part of the state's urban mortgages were in

New York City, so that the New York state mortgage rate quoted is dominated by the New York City rates.

19. See, for example, Willis, *Federal Reserve Bank of San Francisco*, 21.
20. See Remi Nadeau, *Los Angeles: From Mission to Modern City* (New York: Longmans, Green, and Co., 1960), 75.
21. The boom was looked upon with disfavor by the more staid financiers of San Francisco.
22. Lynn Pierson Doti, "Banking in California: Some Evidence on Structure 1878-1905" (Ph.D. diss., University of California at Riverside, 1978).
23. Frederiksen, "Mortgage Banking", 213, found in an 1891 New York report, that of 167 mortgage companies listed, five were in Washington state; none were listed in California or Oregon. The Midwestern mortgage company is well-researched in Allan Bogue, *Money at Interest* (Ithaca: Cornell University Press, 1955).
24. See Nash, *State Government and Economic Development*; Bean, *California: An Interpretive History*.
25. Doti, "Banking in California."
26. See Joseph Crumb, "Banking Regulation in California," 31-32.
27. Richard Keehn and Gene Smiley, "Mortgage Lending by National Banks," *Business History Review* 51 (Winter 1977), 478.
28. See James, *Money and Capital Markets*, 59-64.
29. Keehn and Smiley, "Mortgage Lending," 485. These figures may seem low, but it must be remembered that these are loans in direct violation of the real estate mortgage provision and do not include loan renewals secured by mortgages.
30. Keehn and Smiley, "Mortgage Lending," 488.
31. Eugene White, *Regulation and Reform*, 12.
32. See Cross, *Financing an Empire*, 324, 834-835.
33. The personal correspondence of William Chapman Ralston in the Bancroft Library at the University of California contains a number of letters from Comptroller of the Currency Knox, urging Ralston to lead the way in transferring his bank to a national charter.
34. George Barnett, *State Banks and Trust Companies* (Washington, D.C.: Government Printing Office, 1911), 224.

35. Many authors have used available state bank data to analyze financial market activity within a single state. These include Richard Keehn, "Federal Bank Policy, Bank Market Structure, and Bank Performance: Wisconsin, 1863-1914," *Business History Review* 48 (Spring 1974); Doti, "Banking in California," and Roger Lister, "Bank Behavior, Regulation, and Economic Development: California, 1860-1910" (Ph.D. diss., University of California [Davis], 1982).

36. Authors such as Davis, "The Investment Market," Richard Sylla, "Federal Policy, Banking Market Structure, and Sushka and Barrett, "Banking Structure," aggregate data before analyzing it; others (Smiley, "Evolution and Structure," James, "Evolution of the National Money Market") aggregate states when drawing their conclusions from the data.

37. Davis, "The Investment Market," 337.

38. See, for example, the discussion in Gene Smiley, "The Evolution and Structure of the National Banking System, 1870-1913" (Ph.D. diss., University of Iowa, 1973) and John James, "Evolution of the National Money Market."

39. Professor James generously agreed to share his raw data and calculated interest rate series with me.

40. David Alhadeff, *Monopoly and Competition in Banking* (Berkeley: University of California Press, 1954) presents an excellent discussion of the relative size of the banking market faced by firms; this size varies with the size of the firm. Even today, most firms face, at most, a banking market of regional size; only the largest firms can negotiate loans on a nationwide basis.

41. Because of the redefinition of semi-annual periods in 1906, 1907:1 covers September 1906 to January 1907, while 1907:2 covers January 1907 to July 1907, and so on.

42. James, "Evolution of the National Money Market," 399-403.

43. James, *Money and Capital Markets*, 249-250. Smiley, "Evolution and Structure," makes a similar assumption in his interest rate proxy.

44. James, *Money and Capital Markets*, 251. In the Pacific Coast region, demand loans rather than time loans predominated, but loan renewals were high, essentially creating a longer term loan out of a demand loan.

45. Losses and premiums charged off were lumped together in the income statements, but James separated the dollar figure of losses from that of premiums by using the average ratio of losses to the total of losses and premiums reported by the Comptroller in 1885-1887. See John James, "Banking Market Structure, Risk, and the Pattern of Local Interest Rates in the United States, 1893-1911," *Review of Economics and Statistics* 58 (November 1976), 462.
46. Markets which have few participants are more likely to experience large swings in rates in response to individuals' behavior than are markets with large numbers of participants.
47. The Sushka and Barrett, "Banking Structure" paper seems to be one of the few exceptions.
48. George Stigler, "Imperfections in the Capital Market," *Journal of Political Economy* 75 (June 1967), 287-292.
49. Robert Keleher, "Regional Credit Market Integration: A Survey and Empirical Examination" (Working Paper Series, Federal Reserve Bank of Atlanta, 1979), 27.
50. See Keleher, "Regional Credit Market Integration," for an excellent review of this issue in domestic and international capital market literature.
51. Lance Davis, "Capital Immobilities, Institutional Adaptation and Financial Development: The United States and England: An International Comparison," *Zeitschrift für die gesamte Staatswissenschaft* 124 (February 1968), 19.
52. Sushka and Barrett, "Banking Structure," 465; my emphasis.
53. A similar specification, using interest rate levels, is suggested by Keleher, "Regional Credit Market Integration," 35, in his study of contemporary bank loan markets.
54. Marie Sushka and Brian Barrett, "Banking Structure and the National Capital Market, 1869-1914" (Working Paper, Georgia Institute of Technology, Atlanta, September 1983), 21.
55. In fact, capital does not have to physically move between the areas. If the assets in question are seen as equal substitutes for a third asset common to both areas, the rates on these two assets will be coordinated. See Keleher, "Regional Credit Market Integration," 36-38, and Davis, "Capital Immobilities," 19-22, for further discussion.

56. Since the analysis here will compare the Pacific Coast hinterland to both San Francisco and to New York City, we will be able to distinguish between national and regional business cycle explanations. When *b* is the coefficient on SFO, regional business cycles may be the alternative explanation. When *b* is the coefficient on NYC, national business cycles will have to be considered.
57. Keleher's level tests using contemporary rates on more homogeneous short-term bank loans gave intercepts (*a*) ranging from -1.85 to 2.33 and slopes (*b*) of 0.76 to 1.22 for loans of $1000 to $9000 in amount. Keleher, "Regional Credit Market Integration," 66.
58. Few if any previous studies using this data have accounted for this discontinuity in the series; the "jump" seen in state rates around 1900 may be explained by the establishment of many new reserve cities, whose removal from country bank rates causes these redefined rates to suddenly increase.
59. The possibility that Portland did not develop networks into Oregon is seen in the fact that, in 1893, only 37 percent of Oregon banks chose a Portland correspondent.
60. All subsequent Oregon regressions will present results which include the reserve dummy as a regressor.
61. It is interesting to note that, by including the convergence variable, "ln time," the sensitivity of Chicago rates to New York City becomes more obvious, since the coefficient *b* now equals 0.367, and is statistically significant. It is possible that the downward trend of Chicago rates was so pronounced compared to New York's relatively flat trend that movements about the trend were swamped and did not show up in the first simple regressions.
62. Recall the discussion in Davis, "Capital Immobilities," about the possibility of differentials declining without capital actually flowing from low interest to high interest area.
63. See Charles Kindleberger, *Manias, Panics, and Crashes* (London: Macmillan Press, 1978).
64. Harry Scheiber et al., [*American Economic History* (New York: Harper & Row, 1976), 233], date the depression as 1893-1897; Milton Friedman and Anna Jacobson Schwartz [*A Monetary History of the United States, 1867-1960* (Princeton:

Princeton University Press, 1963), 113] put the trough at June 1897.

65. For example, Cross, [*Financing an Empire*, 588] claims that it took until 1877 for the panic of 1873 to reach California, which suggests an entirely separate business cycle rather than an implausible five-year lag.

66. See Morton Rothstein, "The California 'Wheat Kings'" (Working Paper #22, Agricultural History Center, University of California [Davis], July 1985), 16.

67. Tattersall, "Economic Development of the Pacific Northwest," 163.

68. Kindleberger [*Economic Response*, 66-125] sees this lender of last resort function for areas experiencing liquidity problems as a key responsibility of any financial leader.

69. David Baerncopf, "Regional Interest Rates: Municipal Bonds in California, 1900-1957" (Ph.D. diss., Stanford University, 1961), 181.

70. This may be due to the spikiness of the data, and to the periodicity of the data which makes it impossible to match exact timing of the events with the semi-annual September-March and March-September interest rates.

71. For example, if panic or depression resulted in changing estimates of riskiness or higher transactions costs, funds would not flow smoothly between areas in response to interest differentials.

72. Indeed, a perusal of banking texts of the period, such as Edgar Alcorn, *The Duties and Liabilities of Bank Directors* (Columbus, Ohio: Financial Publishing, 1908) or William Kniffin, *The Practical Work of a Bank*, 9th edition (Cambridge: Bankers Publishing Company, 1948) gives one some uneasiness about the whole of bank accounting practices for expenses and earnings.

73. Smiley, "Evolution and Structure," 508-510.

74. This *assumes* the sort of financial regionality that I am trying to verify and measure in this research.

75. Smiley, "Evolution and Structure," 544-546.

76. James, "Evolution of the National Money Market," 423-424.

77. Friedman and Schwartz, *Monetary History of the United States*, 108, claim that the deflation of the 1890s almost guaranteed that assets would be sold at a loss from book value.
78. Friedman and Schwartz, *Monetary History of the United States*, 148-149, note a mild business recession beginning in June 1899 and the outbreak of the Boer War in October 1899: "There followed a monetary stringency in the fall of 1899, a panic in the stock market, and a number of failures of banks and financial institutions."
79. The rather low R^2 (meaning that a small proportion of interest rate variability can be attributed to the movements in the San Francisco rate) do suggest that local shocks were also important determinants of local rates. The magnitude of the R^2 also reflect the spikiness of the interest rate proxies, so that low R^2 levels cannot be completely attributed to lack of influence of the San Francisco rate movement.

CHAPTER 7

Conjectures and Conclusions

While most discussions of capital mobilization in American economic history rest upon comparisons of interest rates averaged over broad regions, this work has investigated the mobilization of capital *within* the Pacific Coast region between 1850 and 1920. The historical record and empirical results presented here give clear evidence of San Francisco's financial leadership of the dynamic Pacific Coast region in the late nineteenth and early twentieth centuries. This regional market lessened the burden of isolation from New York City and also laid the foundation for eventual integration of the region into a national capital market--a market in which San Francisco was to become one of the three primary American financial centers.

The motivation for this study of region-level financial relationships is a conceptual framework in which complete capital market integration occurs through the linkage of regional markets. These regional markets connect city centers to hinterlands; interregional flows of capital to the city centers will not constitute national capital market formation unless regional markets can then distribute the funds throughout the hinterland. Furthermore, if a region is isolated from national financial markets, the efficiency of the internal financial market will be crucial to the growth and development of the region.

Massive immigration into the three states of the developing Pacific Coast region resulted in an increase in population double that of any other area between 1880 and 1920.[1] And yet, per capita income levels in the Pacific Coast region were higher than in any other region during the same period.[2] The framework developed in this research has suggested that the success of the Pacific Coast region can be partly attributed to its ability to mobilize home savings to new projects in the area, and to supply an increasing labor force with capital.

This evidence may be contrasted with the situation in the southern United States before the depression of the 1930s. Despite net migration from the South Atlantic and East South Central regions, per capita income levels in those regions were little more than half the national average between 1880 and 1920.[3] There were, however, opportunities for growth in the region; estimates of manufacturing rates of return in 1860 exceeded 28 percent,[4] and agricultural returns in 1899 were at least twelve percent.[5] It would seem that, even if the local population of the South had low levels of savings,[6] the high rates of return available in the region would have promoted efficient use of available home savings, and attracted inflows of capital from nearby northeastern financial centers. We should have seen a rapid reduction in southern rates of return. However, southern interest rates were far higher than any eastern rates in the late nineteenth century, and large interest differentials persisted into the 1920s, when interest rates in most other regions had fallen to the eastern level.

The national capital market literature, which couches most explanations in terms of interregional barriers to capital flows, finds this result puzzling. We can reconcile relative southern proximity to New York City with failure to "integrate" into the national market by appealing to the framework that has been developed in this study. If no internal financial market existed in the South, then proximity to eastern financial centers, and low costs of funds transfer to major cities of the South (low "interregional costs") would not reduce average regional interest rates because the funds could not be mobilized throughout the region. The high costs of internal funds transfer would also discourage capital imports by raising total costs of lending in the South. Finally, local savings would be inefficiently utilized. The net effect of absence of regional markets would be a type of isolation from the national market, and delay of integration into that market. Seen within this framework, it is clear why the South stagnated.

This approach is more appealing and complete than most previous work which has difficulty reconciling the South's proximity to New York City with its inability to attach to the national market. Davis tries to explain the puzzle by suggesting that there was a lack of "saver education" in the South.[7] James develops an hypothesis which comes closer to the one presented here. He claims that

> (i)nstitutions did exist to facilitate the flow of funds from outside into the southern financial system. They constitute a de facto case that capital mobility was possible. Barriers to interregional flows of funds were not prohibitively high. The major explanation for retarded southern financial development has to be sought in factors *internal* to the southern capital market. . . .[8]

James ultimately pins the blame for high interest rates and financial underdevelopment on local banking monopoly power, which persisted in this region of low population density and low urbanization. He notes that the key feature of low population density in the South (as opposed to the West) was the lack of small towns. James concludes that, if transactions costs increased with distance, banking markets would be very limited in the region and, at most, only one bank could be supported in any given area. The consequence was monopoly interest rates.[9]

While James emphasizes the local monopoly power of banks in areas of highly dispersed population, the conceptual framework here emphasizes the barriers to commercial and financial network-building which result in part from low population density and lack of urban hierarchy. The commercial patterns of the antebellum South put severe restrictions on the networks which form the basis for financial markets. After the Civil War, the new economic patterns which arose were partly a response to lack of a regional financial market, and partly a cause of continuing financial underdevelopment.

Before the Civil War, the major entrepôt of New Orleans was an outward-looking seaport city, which collected cotton for shipment. New Orleans had very little internally-directed trade, and did not perform the role of industrial center in producing import-substituting goods or in processing raw materials.[10] The antebellum factoring system which was headquartered in New York City provided for the commercial and financial needs of the planter class;[11] poorer residents relied on mercantile credit from local stores, when they could get any credit at all. Thus, the commercial networks, which usually provide information on financial opportunities, were underdeveloped; the incentives for individuals to collect financial information were limited in this one-crop economy.

There were many consequences for formation of antebellum regional financial markets. Large savers put funds into slave capital rather than financial capital. Large borrowers tended to look to a center outside the region (New York City) for funds while small investors either went without funds or sought funds from local merchants. No internal market centered on the New Orleans metropolis developed. This may be contrasted with the foundations of the Pacific Coast regional market, in which commercial and financial networks converged on San Francisco, where large accumulations of liquid mercantile profits sought regional investment opportunities.

The Civil War destroyed the plantation system which had been the basis for the efficient factoring links between the South and New York City. The sharecropping system which evolved in the late 1800s, with large numbers of small borrowers having no credit history, was incompatible with the factoring organization. However, no alternative financial structure was available to small farmers, tenants, and sharecroppers. As a result, these producers were forced to seek finance from local merchants, at monopoly rates.[12] Industrial projects were also limited to local savings supplies; textile mills built in the 1870s were financed by local residents who considered the mills a possible source of local growth.[13] The capital that did flow into the textile industry from the northeast came in the form of direct investment--the transfer of textile capital from eastern firms into southern branches of their companies--not in portfolio investment through financial markets.[14]

All of these observations can be explained by the absence of a regional market in the South. Local monopoly power of isolated institutions; self-financed investment, or investment funds raised locally; and direct investment by outside investors in familiar industries are all hallmarks of undeveloped internal financial markets. All involve high costs and inefficiencies which would be erased if markets were in place.

Gavin Wright suggests that the South comprised an isolated labor market;[15] the inability or unwillingness of labor to migrate kept wages and per capita incomes low in the face of large natural population increases. The apparent absence of *financial markets* in that region compounded low labor productivity by making it very difficult to attract and mobilize capital with which to maintain or raise the productivity of the labor force. The South's fate was sealed--it stagnated until the federal government stepped in during the depression of the 1930s. Wright outlines the transition of the Southern labor market; more work needs to be done on the causes of and remedies for Southern financial backwardness during this period. Such research in economic history has a current application. It might provide clues to the causes of and remedies for underdevelopment and stagnation in poorer developing countries today.

NOTES

1. Richard Easterlin, "Regional Growth of Income" in Simon Kuznets and Dorothy Swaine Thomas, eds., *Population Redistribution and Economic Growth, United States, 1870-1950*, II (Philadelphia: American Philosophical Society, 1960), 171. This conclusion excepts the Mountain region (the Rocky Mountain states and the desert states), whose population increase almost equalled that of the Pacific, but which started from a much smaller base in 1880.
2. Easterlin, "Regional Growth of Income," 146.
3. Easterlin, "Regional Growth of Income," 146, 171. The South Atlantic and the East South Central regions include states east of the Mississippi River and south of the Ohio River.
4. Fred Bateman and Thomas Weiss, *A Deplorable Scarcity* (Chapel Hill: University of North Carolina Press, 1981), 116.
5. Fogel and Rutner, "Efficiency Effects of Federal Land Policy," 398.
6. This is likely before the Civil War; Ransom and Sutch have argued that slaveowners were not life cycle savers. Roger Ransom and Richard Sutch "Domestic Saving as an Active Constraint on Capital Formation in the American Economy, 1839-1928: A Provisonal Theory" (Working Papers on the History of Saving, #1. Berkeley: Institute of Business and Economic Research, December 1984). After the Civil War, the high proportion of farmers at the poverty level would reduce total savings in the region.
7. Davis, "Capital Immobilities and Finance Capitalism: A Study of Economic Evolution in the United States 1820-1920," *Explorations in Entrepreneurial History* 1 (Fall 1963), 97.
8. John James, "Financial Underdevelopment in the Postbellum South," *Journal of Interdisciplinary History* 11 (Winter 1981), 446-447; my emphasis.
9. James, "Financial Underdevelopment," 450-451.
10. See Pred, *Spatial Dynamics of U.S. Urban-Industrial Growth*; Jacobs, *Cities and the Wealth of Nations*.
11. Lewis Atherton, *The Southern Country Store 1800-1860* (Baton Rouge: Louisiana State University Press, 1949).

12. This issue is well-researched in Roger Ransom and Richard Sutch, *One Kind of Freedom: The Economic Consequences of Emancipation* (Cambridge: Cambridge University Press, 1977).
13. Lance Davis, "Comment," *Second International Conference of Economic History: Aix-en-Provence, 1962*, vol. II (Paris: Mouton, 1965), 662.
14. Davis, "The Investment Market," 391; Gavin Wright, *Old South, New South* (New York: Basic Books, 1986), 135-147.
15. Wright, *Old South, New South.*

APPENDIX OF FIGURES

FIGURE 2.1

COMPTROLLER OF THE CURRENCY REGIONAL DEFINITIONS

Region I	Region II	Region III
Maine	New York	Virginia
Vermont	New Jersey	West Virgina
New Hampshire	Pennsylvania	North Carolina
Massachusetts	Delaware	South Carolina
Rhode Island	Maryland	Georgia
Connecticut	District of Columbia	Florida
		Alabama
		Mississippi
		Louisiana
		Texas
		Arkansas
		Kentucky
		Tennessee

Region IV	Region V	Region VI
Ohio	North Dakota	Washington
Indiana	South Dakota	Oregon
Illinois	Nebraska	California
Michigan	Kansas	Arizona
Wisconsin	Montana	Nevada
Minnesota	Wyoming	Idaho
Iowa	Colorado	Utah
Missouri	New Mexico	
	Oklahoma	

FIGURE 6.1

ABBREVIATIONS

Cities

NYC	=	New York City
BOS	=	Boston
CHI	=	Chicago
STL	=	St. Louis
SFO	=	San Francisco

States

NY	=	New York
IL	=	Illinois
MO	=	Missouri
CA	=	California
OR	=	Oregon
WA	=	Washington

Figure 6.2 a

Index of Seasonal Variation
National Bank Deposits

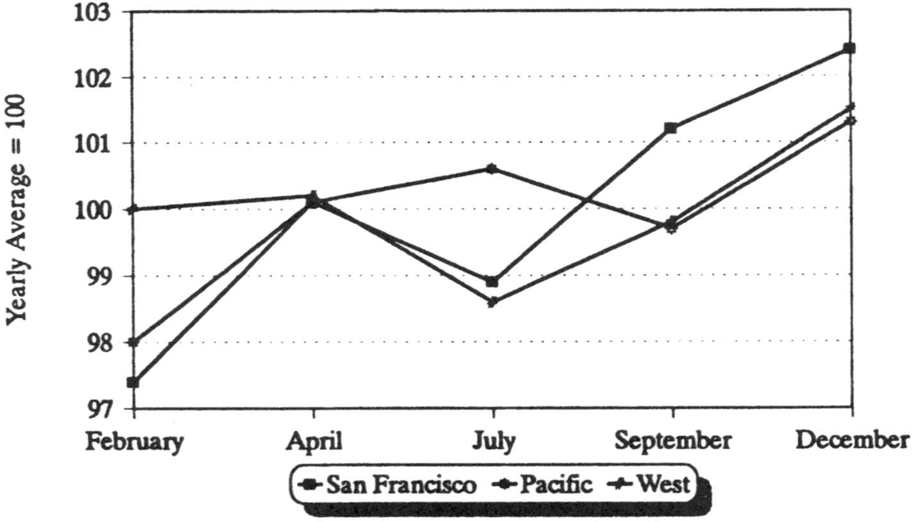

Source: Allyn Young, "An Analysis of Bank Statistics," *Review of Economic Statistics* 7 (April 1925), 87.

Figure 6.2 b

Index of Seasonal Variation
National Bank Loans

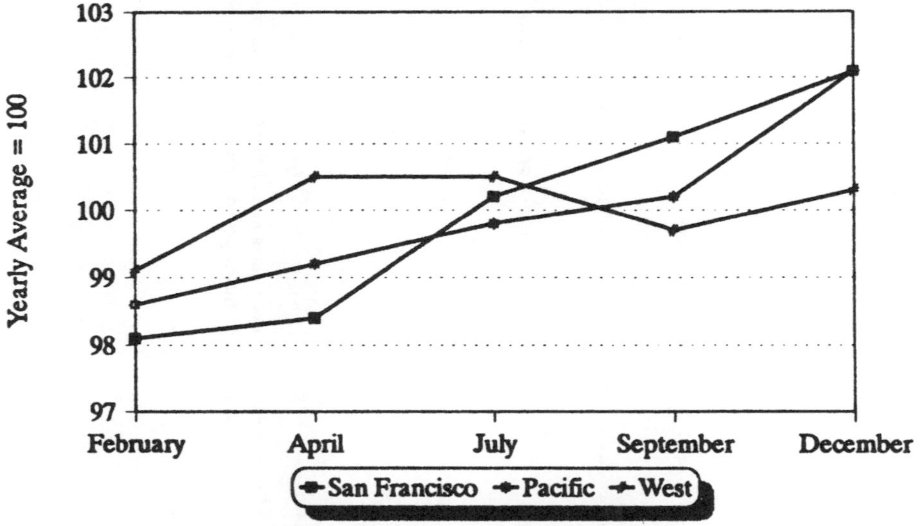

Source: Allyn Young, "An Analysis of Bank Statistics," Review of Economic Statistics 7 (April 1925), 87.

FIGURE 6.3

BRADSTREET'S COMMERCIAL PAPER RATES FOR PACIFIC COAST CITIES, 1894-1904

	1894 1895 1896 1897 1898 1899 1900 1901 1902 1903 1904
SanFrancisco	--------3-4% -------/xxxxxxxx /------- 4-6% ------------ / 5% -------------
LosAngeles	------- 7-9% ----------------- /------- 7-8% ------- /xxxxxxxxxxxxxxx
Portland	----------- 8% --------------- /xxxxxxx /--5%--/ --5-7%--- /xxxxxx
Seattle	------9-11%-------- /------ 8-10% -------- / ---6%---- /xxxxxx

NOTES: Rates listed are the exact quotations of *Bradstreets Journal* for each week of the indicated years. x marks periods when no quotation was given.

Figure 6.4 a

Mortgage Rate on Lots, 1880 - 1889
New York City and Chicago

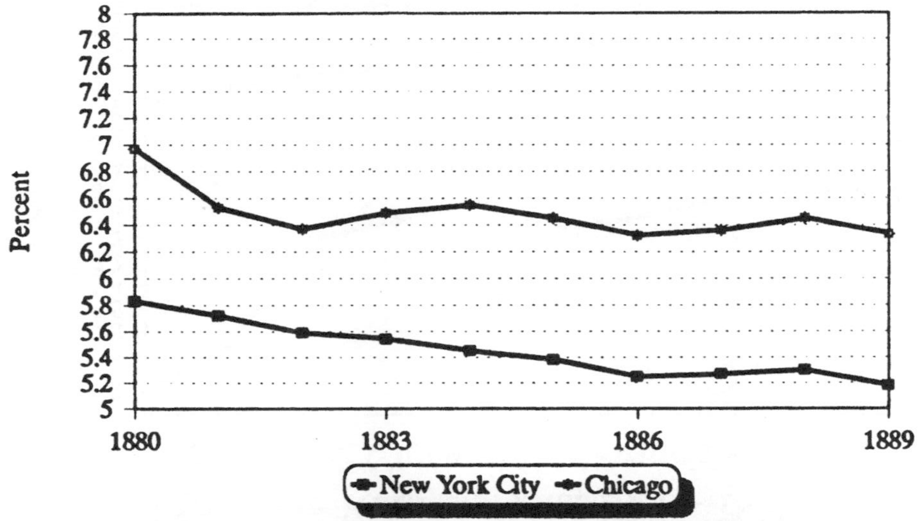

Source: U.S. Census Office, **Report on Real Estate Mortgages in the United States at the Eleventh Census: 1890** (Washington, D.C.: Government Printing Office, 1895) 248-251.

Figure 6.4 b

Mortgage Rate on Lots, 1880 - 1889
New York City and San Francisco

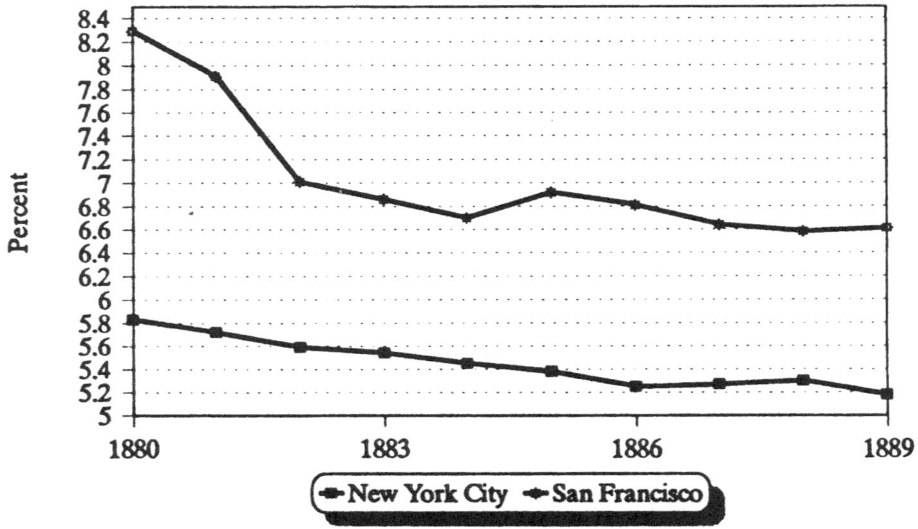

Source: U.S. Census Office, **Report on Real Estate Mortgages in the United States at the Eleventh Census: 1890** (Washington, D.C.: Government Printing Office, 1895) 248-251.

Figure 6.4 c

Mortgage Rate on Lots, 1880 - 1889
Chicago and San Francisco

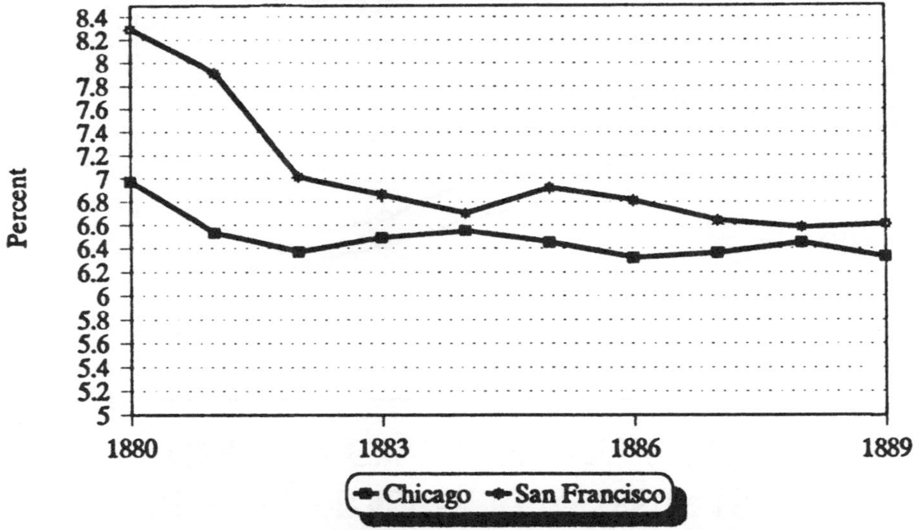

Source: U.S. Census Office, **Report on Real Estate Mortgages in the United States at the Eleventh Census: 1890** (Washington, D.C.: Government Printing Office, 1895) 248-251.

Figure 6.4 d

Mortgage Rate on Lots, 1880 - 1889
New York City and New York State

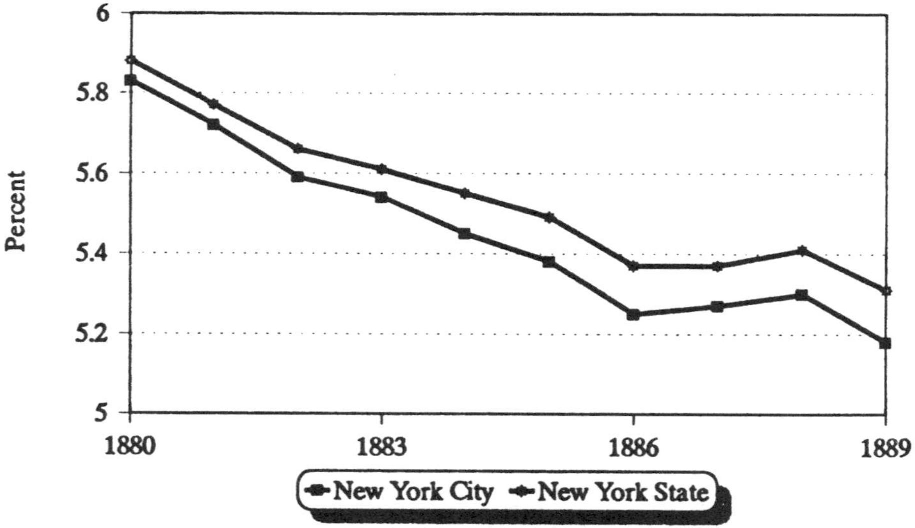

Source: U.S. Census Office, **Report on Real Estate Mortgages in the United States at the Eleventh Census: 1890** (Washington, D.C.: Government Printing Office, 1895) 248-251.

Figure 6.4 e

Mortgage Rate on Lots, 1880 - 1889
Chicago and Illinois

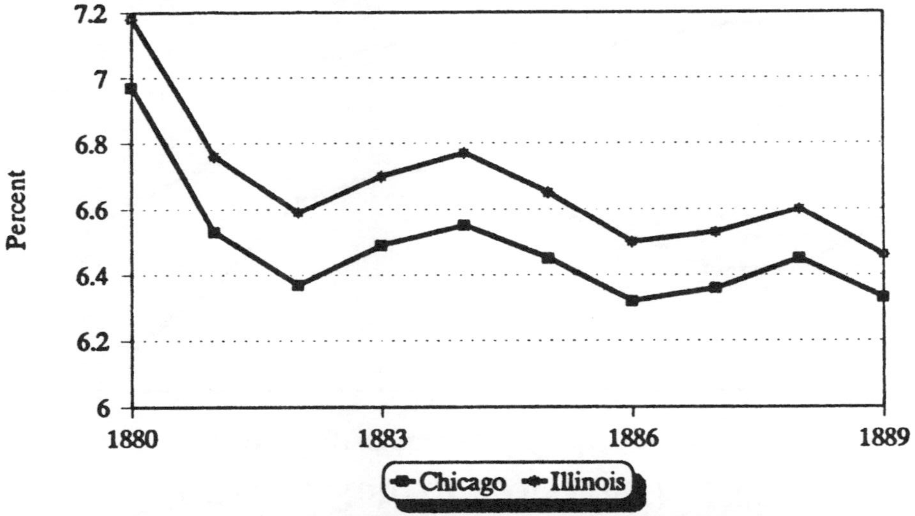

Source: U.S. Census Office, Report on Real Estate Mortgages in the United States at the Eleventh Census: 1890 (Washington, D.C.: Government Printing Office, 1895) 248-251.

Figure 6.4 f

Mortgage Rate on Lots, 1880 - 1889
San Francisco and California

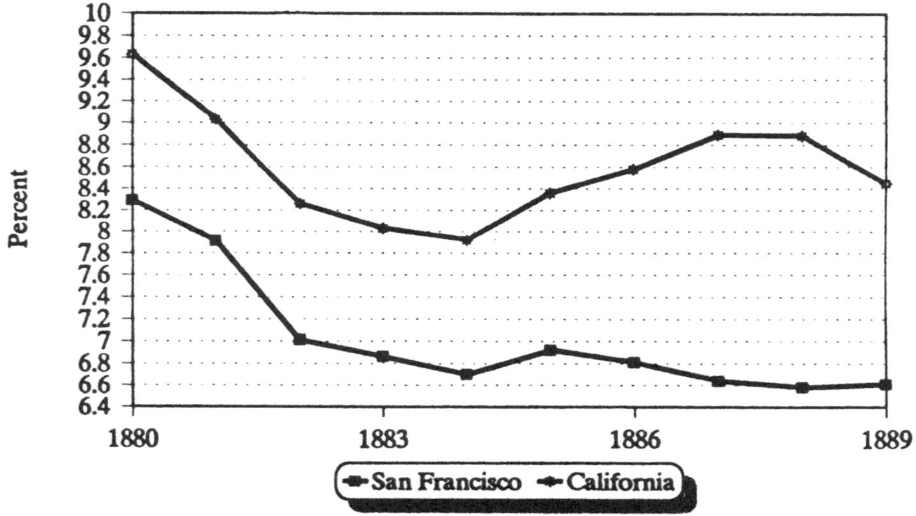

Source: U.S. Census Office, **Report on Real Estate Mortgages in the United States at the Eleventh Census: 1890** (Washington, D.C.: Government Printing Office, 1895) 248-251.

Figure 6.4 g

Mortgage Rate on Lots, 1880 - 1889
San Francisco and Oregon

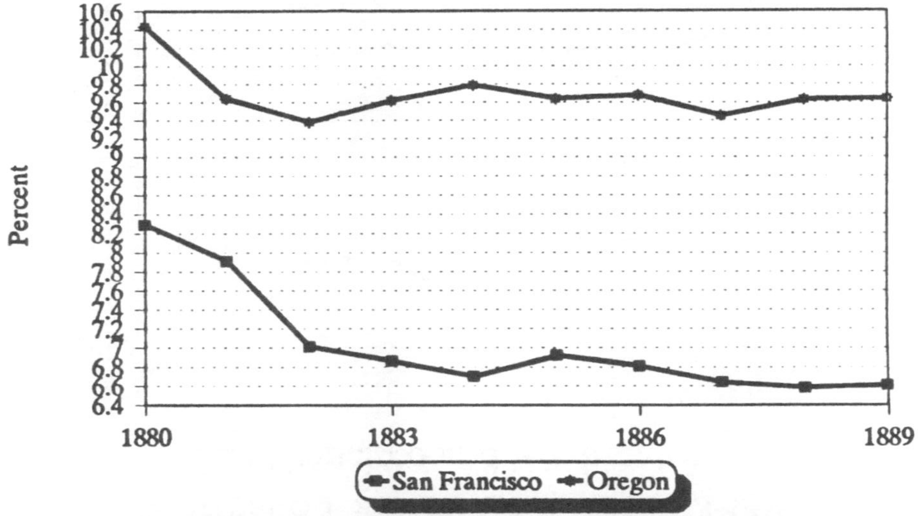

Source: U.S. Census Office, **Report on Real Estate Mortgages in the United States at the Eleventh Census: 1890** (Washington, D.C.: Government Printing Office, 1895) 248-251.

Figure 6.4 h

Mortgage Rate on Lots, 1880 - 1889
San Francisco and Washington

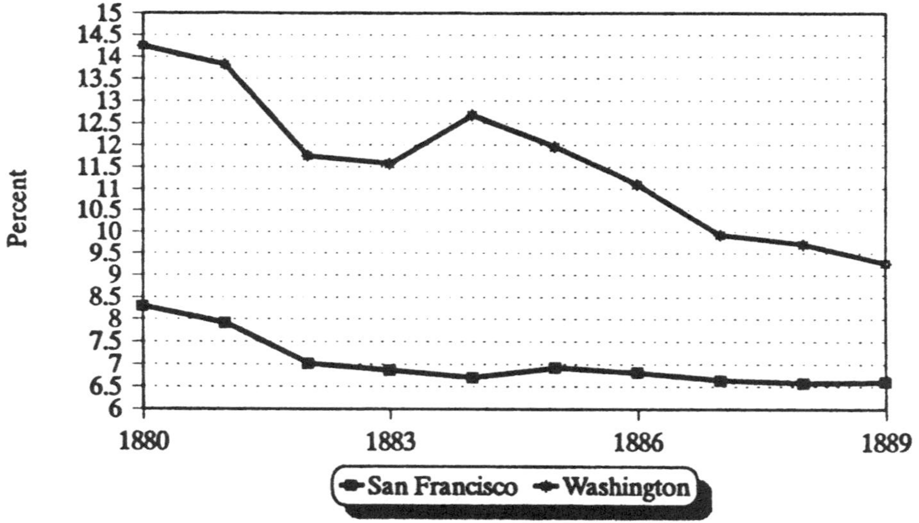

Source: U.S. Census Office, **Report on Real Estate Mortgages in the United States at the Eleventh Census: 1890** (Washington, D.C.: Government Printing Office, 1895) 248-251.

Figure 6.4 i

Mortgage Rates, 1880 - 1889
New York City Lots and New York Acres

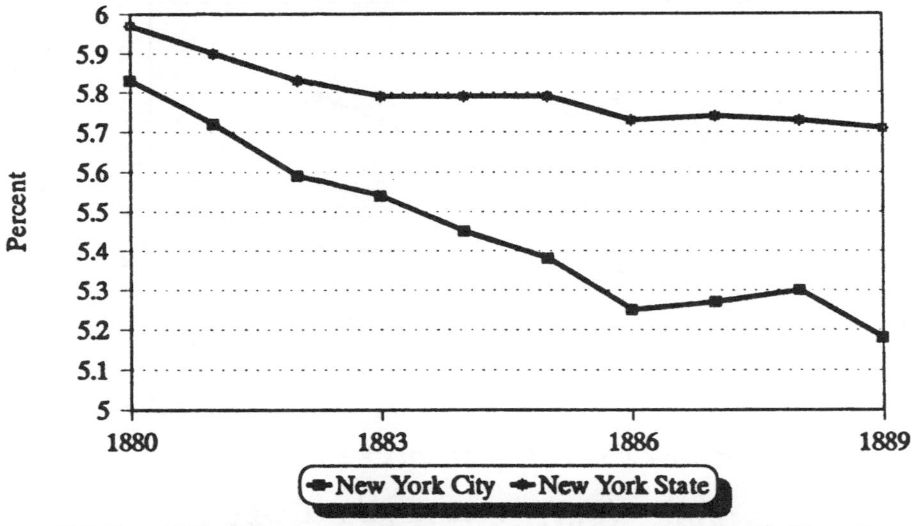

Source: U.S. Census Office, Report on Real Estate Mortgages in the United States at the Eleventh Census: 1890 (Washington, D.C.: Government Printing Office, 1895) 248-251.

Figure 6.4 j

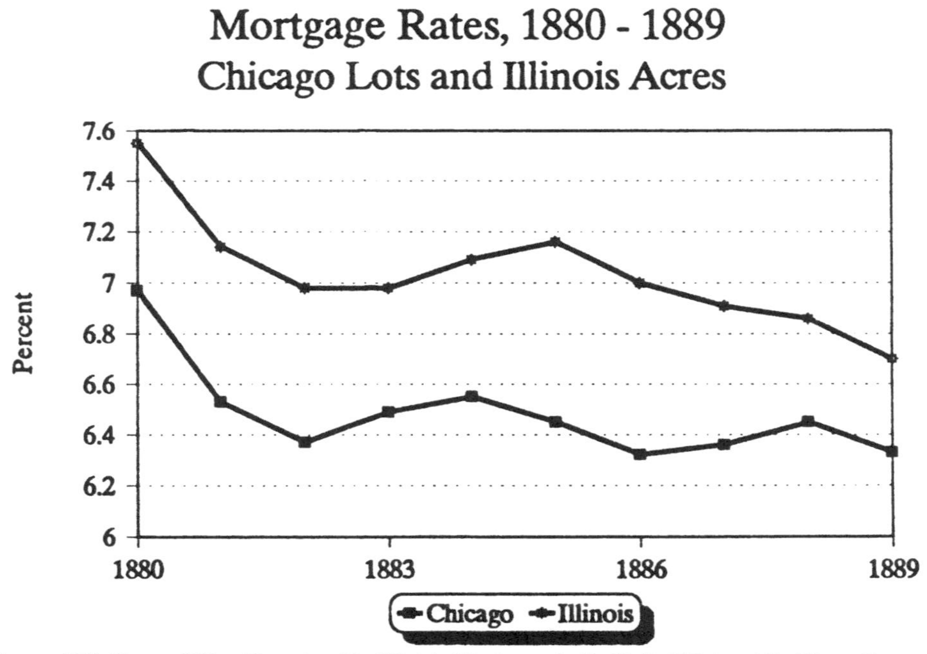

Source: U.S. Census Office, **Report on Real Estate Mortgages in the United States at the Eleventh Census: 1890** (Washington, D.C.: Government Printing Office, 1895) 248-251.

Figure 6.4 k

Mortgage Rates, 1880 - 1889

San Francisco Lots and California Acres

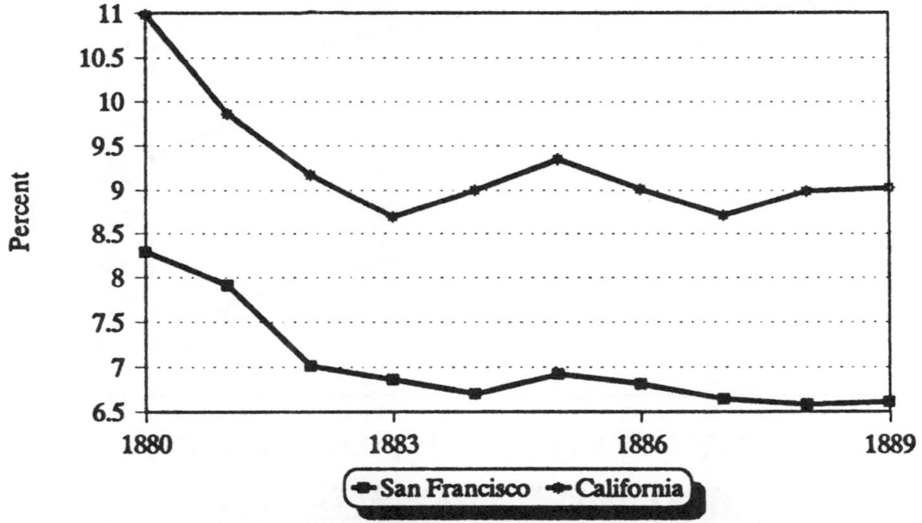

Source: U.S. Census Office, **Report on Real Estate Mortgages in the United States at the Eleventh Census: 1890** (Washington, D.C.: Government Printing Office, 1895) 248-251.

Figure 6.4 1

Mortgage Rates, 1880 - 1889
San Francisco Lots and Oregon Acres

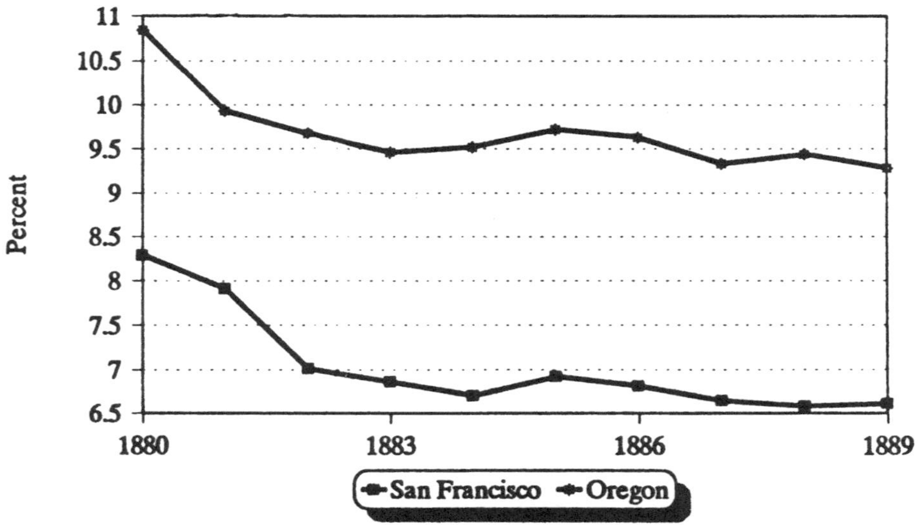

Source: U.S. Census Office, **Report on Real Estate Mortgages in the United States at the Eleventh Census: 1890** (Washington, D.C.: Government Printing Office, 1895) 248-251.

Figure 6.4 m

Mortgage Rates, 1880 - 1889

San Francisco Lots and Washington Acres

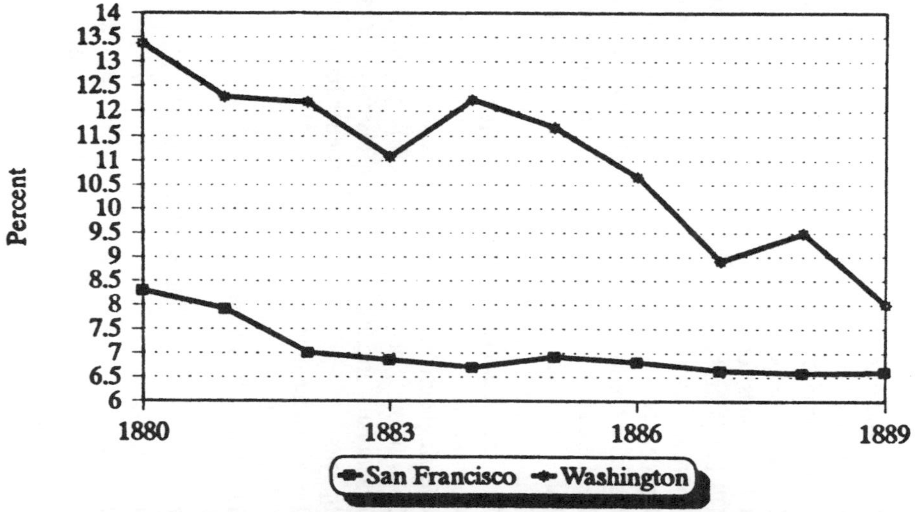

Source: U.S. Census Office, **Report on Real Estate Mortgages in the United States at the Eleventh Census: 1890** (Washington, D.C.: Government Printing Office, 1895) 248-251.

FIGURE 6.5

National Bank Balance Sheet and Income Statement Items

Balance Sheets*

Resources	Liabilities
Loans and discounts	Capital stock
Overdrafts	Surplus fund
Bonds for circulation	Undivided profits
Bonds for deposits	National bank circulation
Other bonds for deposits	State bank circulation
US bonds on hand	Due to national banks
Premiums on bonds	Due to state banks
Bonds, securities	Due to trust companies
Banking house	Due to reserve agents
Real estate	Dividends unpaid
Due from national banks	Individual deposits
Due from state banks	US deposits
Due from reserve agents	Deposits of US disb. ofcrs.
Cash items	Bonds borrowed
Clearinghouse exchanges	Notes rediscounted
Bills of other banks	Bills payable
Fractional currency	Reserved for taxes
Specie	Other liabilities
Legal-tender notes	
5% fund with Treasury	
Due from US Treasury	

Income Statements**

Capital Stock	Losses and premiums charged off
Surplus	Expenses and taxes charged off
Gross earnings	Net earnings
Dividends	

* Balance sheets issued at five "calls" each year.

** Income statements issued semi-annually; gross earnings reported only from 1888 to 1911.

Figure 6.6 a

NewYork City and Boston Earning Rates

Semi-Annual, 1888 to 1911

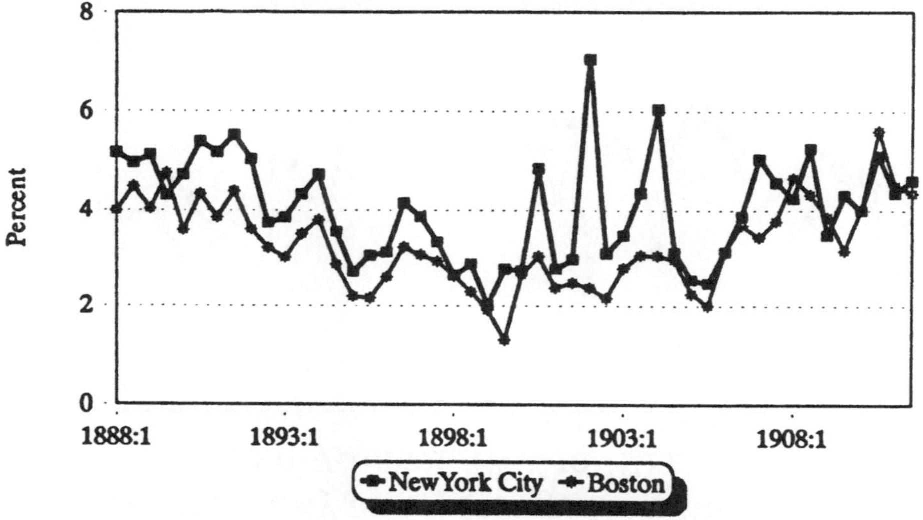

Source: John James, "The Evolution of the National Money Market" (Ph.D. diss., MIT, 1974).

Figure 6.6 b

New York City and Chicago Earning Rates
Semi-Annual, 1888 to 1911

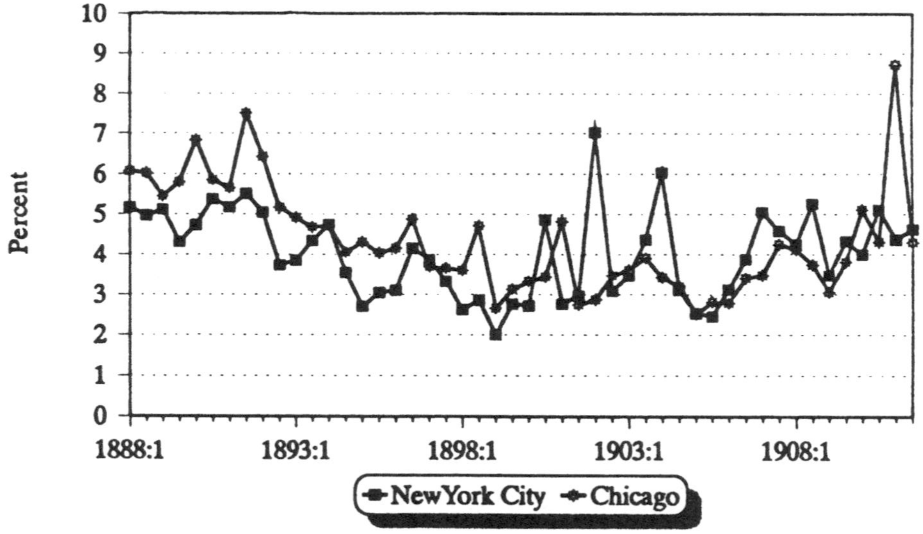

Source: John James, "The Evolution of the National Money Market" (Ph.D. diss., MIT, 1974).

Figure 6.6 c

New York City and San Francisco Earning Rates

Semi-Annual, 1888 to 1911

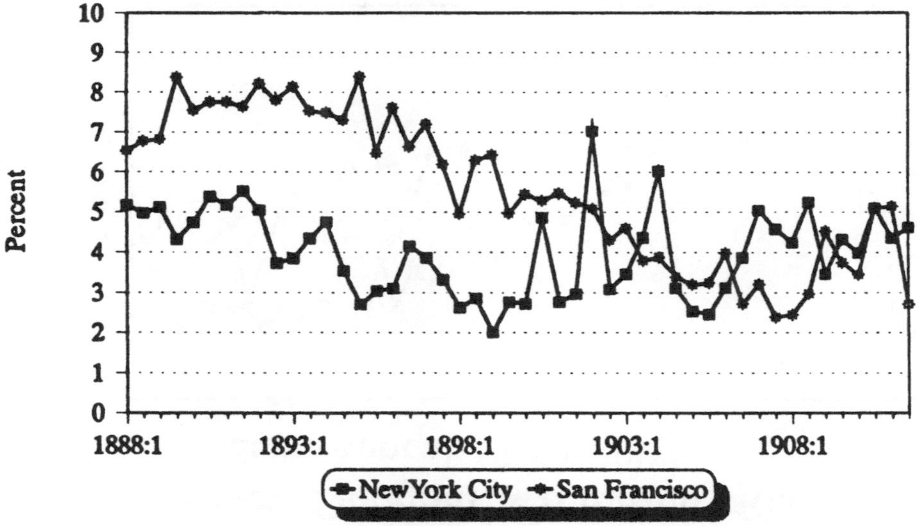

Source: John James, "The Evolution of the National Money Market" (Ph.D. diss., MIT, 1974).

Figure 6.6 d
Chicago and San Francisco Earning Rates
Semi-Annual, 1888 to 1911

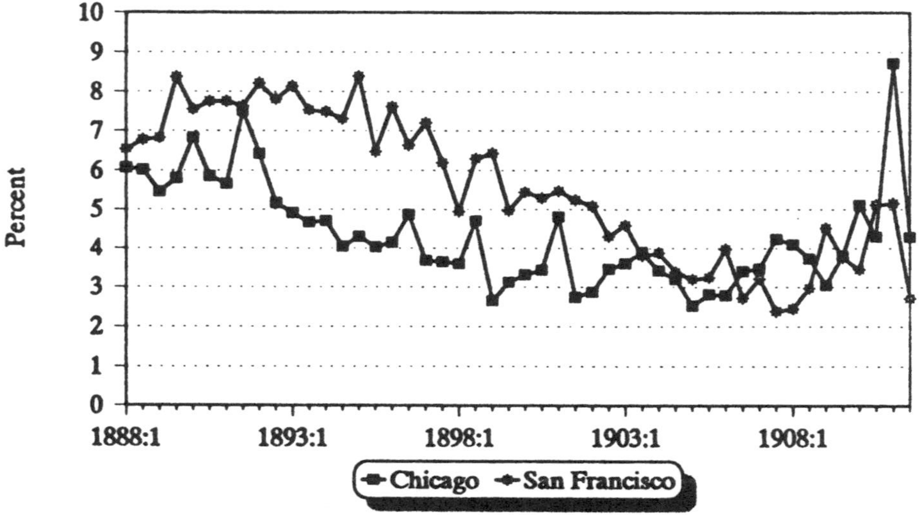

Source: John James, "The Evolution of the National Money Market" (Ph.D. diss., MIT, 1974).

Figure 6.6 e

New York City and New York Earning Rates
Semi-Annual, 1888 to 1911

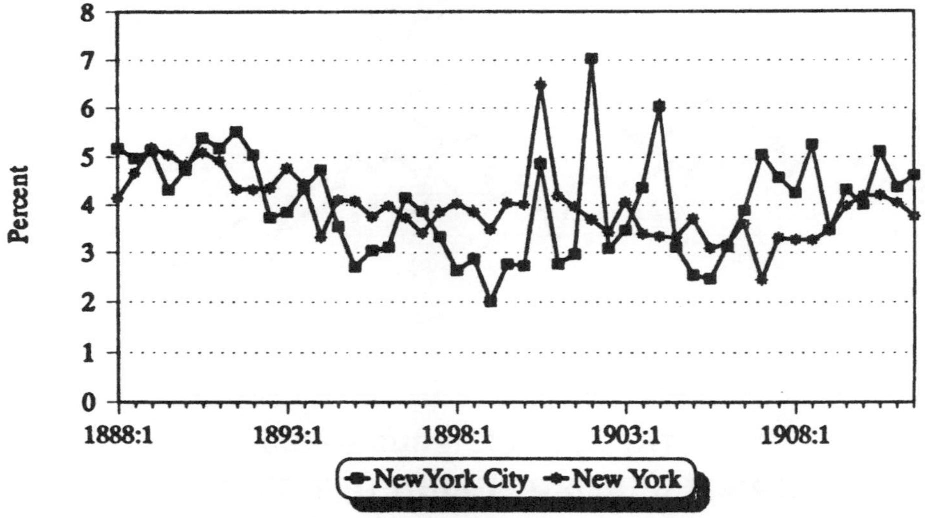

Source: John James, "The Evolution of the National Money Market" (Ph.D. diss., MIT, 1974).

Figure 6.6 f

Chicago and Illinois Earning Rates
Semi-Annual, 1888 to 1911

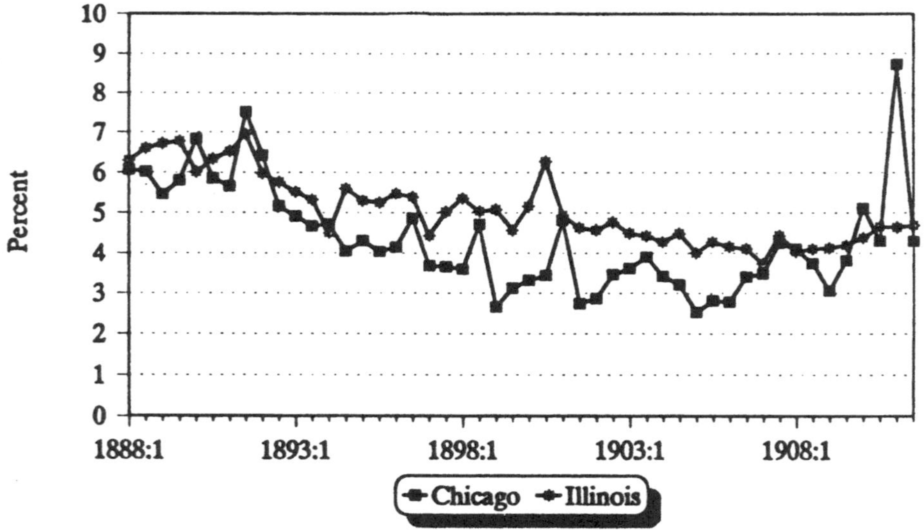

Source: John James, "The Evolution of the National Money Market" (Ph.D. diss., MIT, 1974).

Figure 6.6 g

St. Louis and Missouri Earning Rates
Semi-Annual, 1888 to 1911

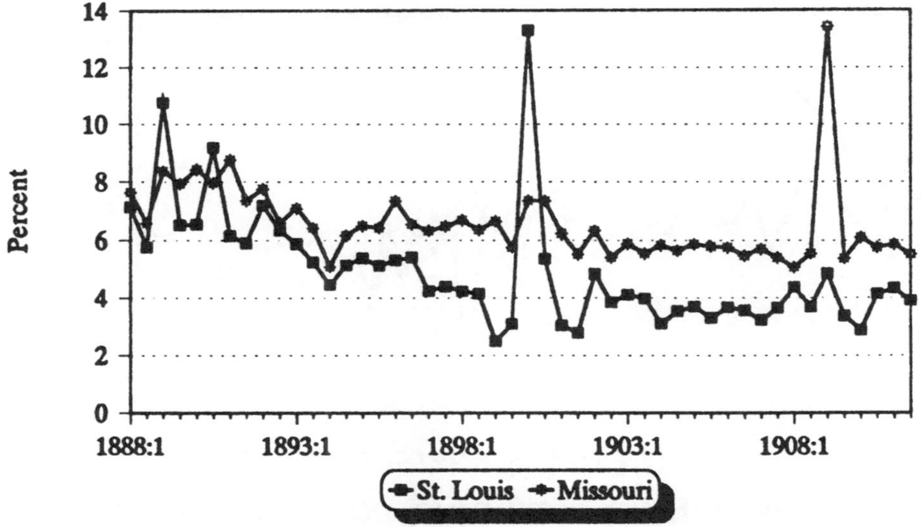

Source: John James, "The Evolution of the National Money Market" (Ph.D. diss., MIT, 1974).

Figure 6.6 h

San Francisco and California Earning Rates

Semi-Annual, 1888 to 1911

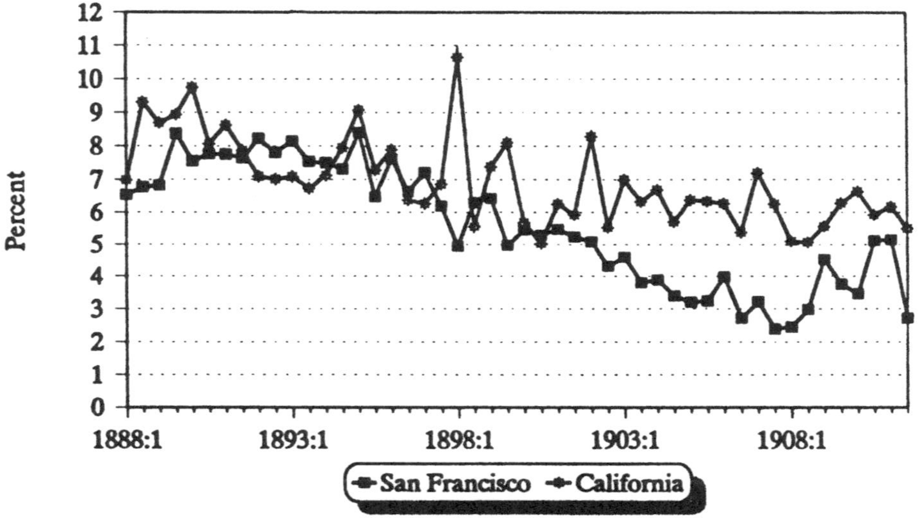

Source: John James, "The Evolution of the National Money Market" (Ph.D. diss., MIT, 1974).

Figure 6.6 i

San Francisco and Oregon Earning Rates
Semi-Annual, 1888 to 1911

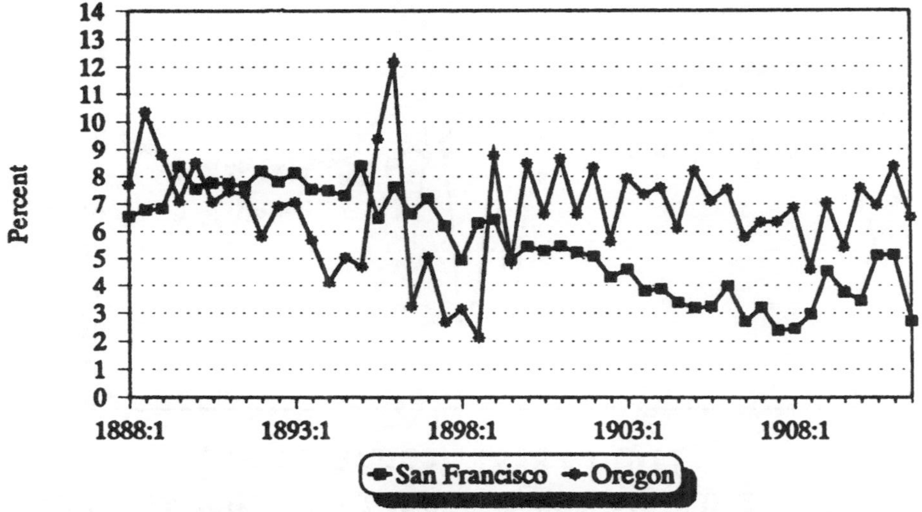

Source: John James, "The Evolution of the National Money Market" (Ph.D. diss., MIT, 1974).

Figure 6.6 j

San Francisco and Washington Earning Rates
Semi-Annual, 1888 to 1911

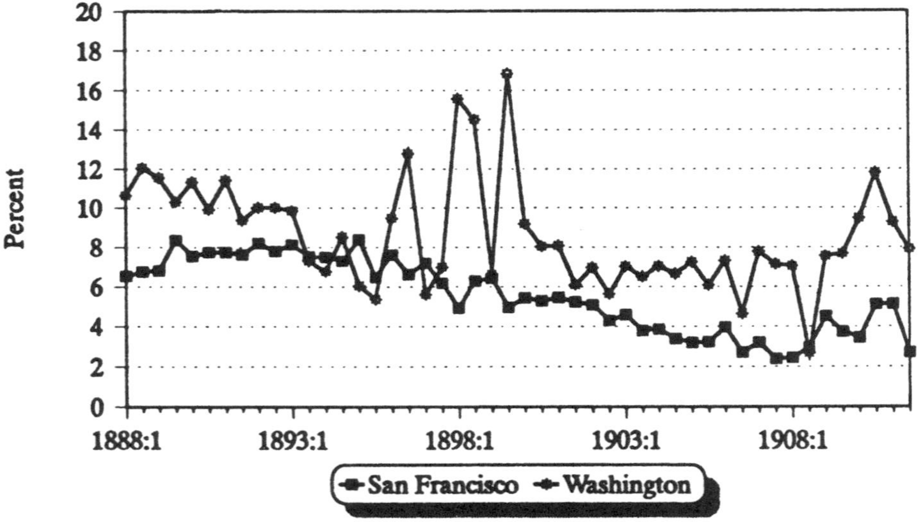

Source: John James, "The Evolution of the National Money Market" (Ph.D. diss., MIT, 1974).

Figure 6.7
Financial Rates, 1888 to 1911

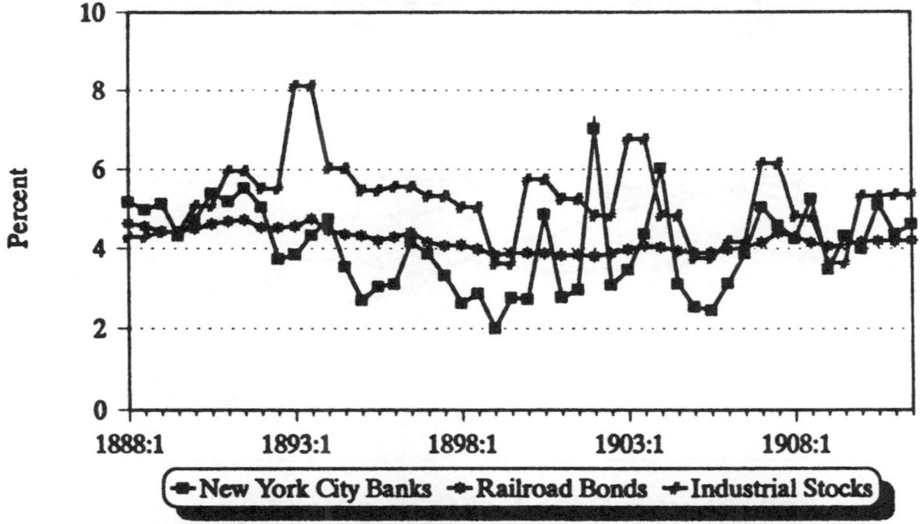

Sources: Bank rates from James, "National Money Market," 1974.
Unadjusted Index of Railroad Bond Yields from Frederick Macaulay, Some Theoretical Problems Suggested by the Movements of Interest Rates (New York: NBER, 1938), A142-A161.
Index of Yields of Industrial Common Stocks from U.S. Bureau of the Census, Historical Statistics of the United States: Colonial Times to 1970 (Washington, D.C.: Government Printing Office, 1975), series X480.

Figure 6.8
National Bank Loans
Depression Years, 1892:2 to 1898:2

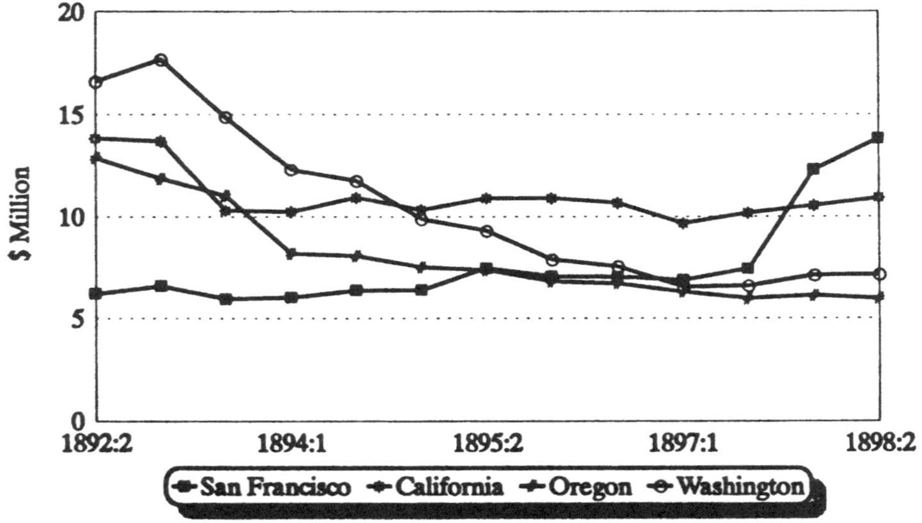

Source: United States Comptroller of the Currency, Annual Reports (Washington, D.C.: Government Printing Office, 1892-1898).

Figure 6.9 a

San Francisco National Bank Gross Earnings
Semi-Annual, 1888 to 1911

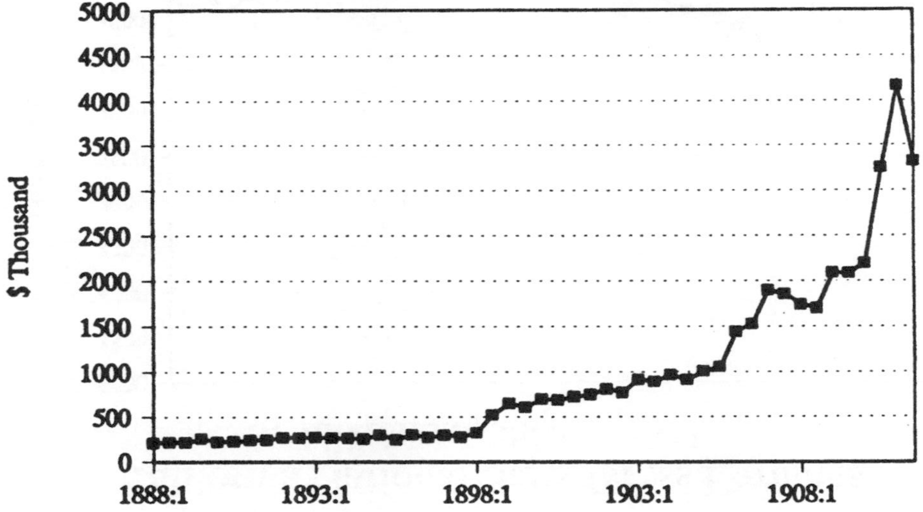

Source: United States Comptroller of the Currency, Annual Reports (1888 - 1911).

Figure 6.9 b

California National Bank Gross Earnings
Semi-Annual, 1888 to 1911

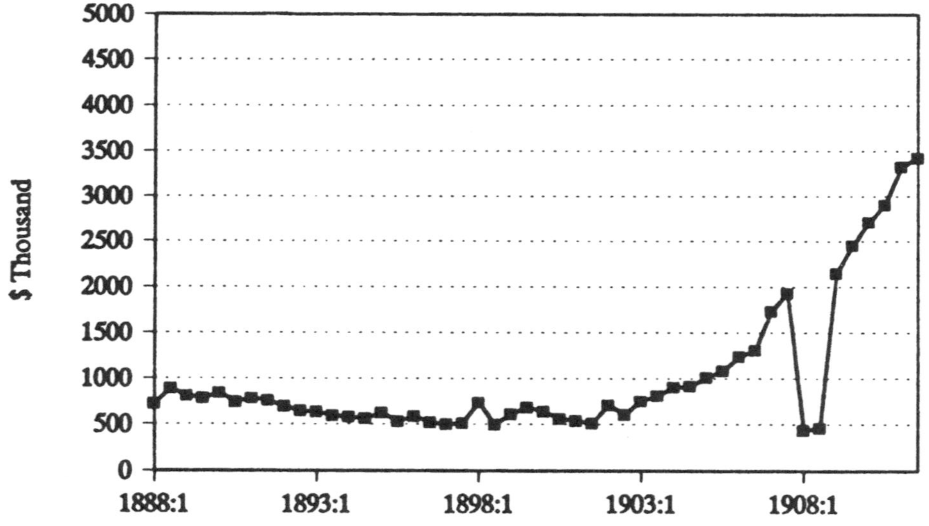

Source: United States Comptroller of the Currency, **Annual Reports** (1888 - 1911).

Figure 6.9 c

Oregon National Bank Gross Earnings

Semi-Annual, 1888 to 1911

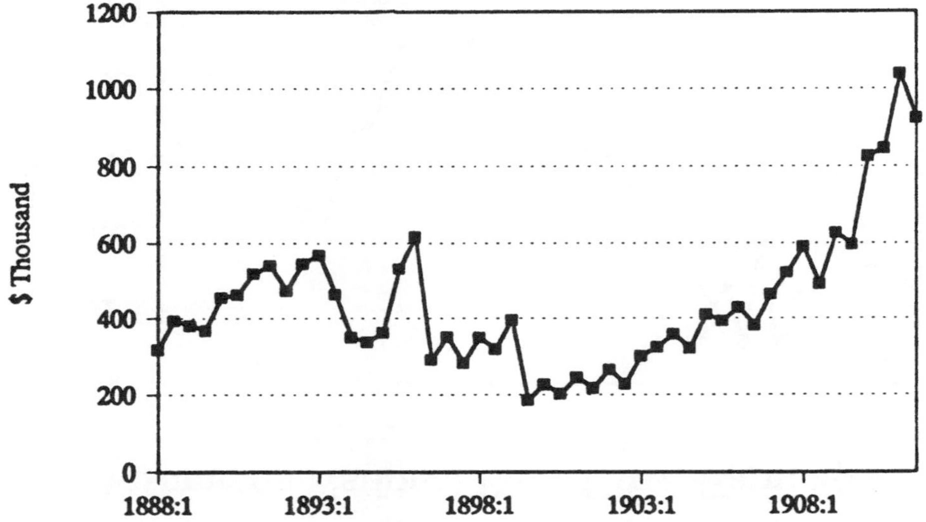

Source: United States Comptroller of the Currency, Annual Reports (1888 - 1911).

Figure 6.9 d

Washington National Bank Gross Earnings
Semi-Annual, 1888 to 1911

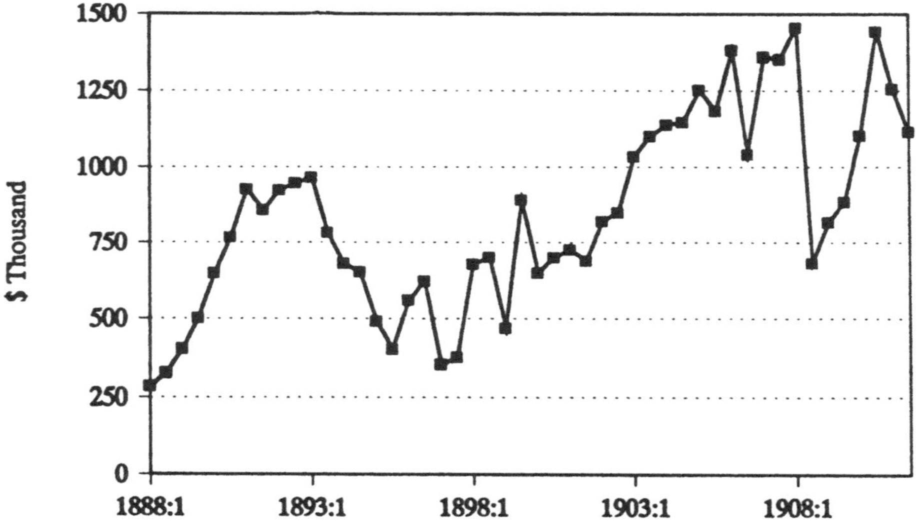

Source: United States Comptroller of the Currency, *Annual Reports* (1888 - 1911).

BIBLIOGRAPHY

Alcorn, Edgar. *The Duties and Liabilities of Bank Directors.* Columbus, Ohio: Financial Publishing, 1908.

Alhadeff, David. *Monopoly and Competition in Banking.* Berkeley: University of California Press, 1954.

Allen, Robert and Donald Watson. *The Structure of the Oregon Economy: An Input/Output Study.* Eugene, Oregon: Bureau of Business and Economic Research, University of Oregon, 1965.

Armstrong, Leroy and J.O. Denny. *Financial California.* San Francisco: Coast Banker Publishing, 1916.

Atack, Jeremy, Fred Bateman and Thomas Weiss. "Risk, the Rate of Return, and the Pattern of Investment in Nineteenth Century American Manufacturing." *Southern Economic Journal* 49 (July 1982): 150-163.

Atherton, Lewis. *The Southern Country Store 1800-1860.* Baton Rouge: Louisiana State University Press, 1949.

Avery, Mary. *Washington: A History of the Evergreen State.* Seattle: University of Washington Press, 1965.

Baerncopf, David. "Regional Interest Rates: Municipal Bonds in California, 1900-1957." Ph.D. dissertation, Stanford University, 1961.

Barnett, George. *State Banks and Trust Companies.* Washington, D.C.: Government Printing Office, 1911.

Barth, Gunther. *Instant Cities: Urbanization and the Rise of San Francisco and Denver.* New York: Oxford University Press, 1975.

Bateman, Fred and Thomas Weiss. *A Deplorable Scarcity.* Chapel Hill: University of North Carolina Press, 1981.

Bean, Walton. *California: An Interpretive History.* New York: McGraw-Hill, 1978.

Berry, Thomas Senior. *Early California: Gold, Prices, Trade.* Richmond, Virginia: The Bostwick Press, 1984.

Blackford, Mansel. "Banking and Bank Legislation in California, 1890-1915." *Business History Review* 47 (Winter 1973): 482-507.

Bogue, Allan. *Money at Interest.* Ithaca: Cornell University Press, 1955.

Bourque, Phillip et al. *The Washington Economy: An Input-Output Study.* Seattle: University of Washington Graduate School of Business Administration, 1967.

Breckenridge, R.M. "Discount Rates in the United States." *Political Science Quarterly* 13 (March 1898): 119-142.

Brewer, H. Peers. "Eastern Money and Western Mortgages in the 1870s." *Business History Review* 50 (Autumn 1976): 356-380.

Broude, Henry. "The Significance of Regional Studies for the Elaboration of National Economic History." *Journal of Economic History* 20 (December 1960): 588-596.

Burt, Ronald and Michael Minor. *Applied Network Analysis.* Beverly Hills: Sage Publications, 1983.

California Board of Bank Commissioners. *Annual Report.* Sacramento: State Printing Office (various years).

Cameron, Rondo, et al. *Banking in the Early Stages of Industrialization.* New York: Oxford University Press, 1967.

Carlton, David and Peter Coclanis. "Capital Mobilization and Southern Industry, 1880-1905: The Case of the Carolina Piedmont." *Journal of Economic History* 49 (March 1989): 73-94.

Carosso, Vincent P. "Proposals for a Regional Financial History of the Middle Atlantic States." in Glenn Porter, ed. *Regional Economic History: The Mid-Atlantic Area since 1700.* Wilmington, Delaware: Eleutherian Mills-Hagley Foundation, 1976.

Cartinhour, Gaines. *Branch, Group and Chain Banking.* New York: Macmillan, 1931.

Caughey, John. *Gold is the Cornerstone.* Berkeley: University of California Press, 1948.

Cleland, Robert and Osgood Hardy. *March of Industry.* Los Angeles: Powell, 1929.

Cleland, Robert and Frank Putnam. *Isaias W. Hellman and the Farmers and Merchants Bank.* San Marino, California: The Huntington Library, 1965.

Code, William R. "The Spatial Dynamics of Financial Intermediaries: An Interpretation of the Distribution of Financial Decision-Making in Canada." Ph.D. dissertation, University of California, 1971.

Cohn, Edwin. *Industry in the Pacific Northwest and the Location Theory.* New York: Kings' Crown Press, 1954.

Coman, Edwin and Helen Gibbs. *Time, Tide and Timber: Over a Century of Pope and Talbot*, revised edition. San Francisco: Pope and Talbot, 1978.

Conzen, Michael. "Capital Flows and the Developing Urban Hierarchy: State Bank Capital in Wisconsin, 1854-1895." *Economic Geography* 51 (October 1975): 321-338.

Conzen, Michael. "The Maturing Urban System in the United States, 1840-1910." *Annals of the Association of American Geographers* 67 (March 1977): 88-108.

Cox, Thomas. *Mills and Markets: A History of the Pacific Coast Lumber Industry to 1900.* Seattle: University of Washington Press, 1974.

Cross, Ira. *Financing an Empire.* Chicago: S.J. Clarke, 1927.

Crumb, Joseph. "Banking Regulation in California." Ph.D. dissertation, University of California, 1935.

Dana, Julian. *The Man Who Built San Francisco.* New York: Macmillan, 1936.

Davis, Lance. "Capital Immobilities and Finance Capitalism: A Study of Economic Evolution in the United States 1820-1920." *Explorations in Entrepreneurial History* 1 (Fall 1963): 88-105.

Davis, Lance. "Capital Immobilities, Institutional Adaptation and Financial Development: The United States and England, An International Comparison." *Zeitschrift für die gesamte Staatswissenschaft* 124 (February 1968): 14-34.

Davis, Lance. "Comment." *Second International Conference of Economic History: Aix-en-Provence, 1962*, vol. II. Paris: Mouton, 1965.

Davis, Lance. "The Investment Market, 1870-1914: The Evolution of a National Market." *Journal of Economic History* 25 (September 1965): 355-399.

Davis, Lance. "The New England Textile Mills and the Capital Markets: A Study of Industrial Borrowing 1840-1860." *Journal of Economic History* 20 (March 1960): 1-30.

Davis, Lance. "United States Financial Intermediaries in the Early Nineteenth Century: Four Case Studies." Ph.D. dissertation, Johns Hopkins University, 1956.

Davis, Lance, Richard Easterlin and William Parker, eds. *American Economic Growth: An Economist's History of the United States.* New York: Harper & Row, 1972.

Davis, Lance and Douglass North. *Institutional Change and American Economic Growth.* Cambridge: Cambridge University Press, 1971.

Davis, Lance and Robert Gallman. "The Share of Savings and Investment in Gross National Product During the 19th Century in the U.S.A." *Fourth International Conference of Economic History: Bloomington, 1968.* Paris: Mouton, 1973.

Davis, Lance and Robert Gallman. "Capital Formation in the United States during the Nineteenth Century." in Peter Mathias and M.M. Postan eds., *The Cambridge Economic History of Europe* vol. VII, pt. 2. Cambridge: Cambridge University Press, 1978.

Dodds, Gordon. *Oregon: A Bicentennial History.* New York: Norton, 1977.

Doti, Lynn Pierson. "Banking in California: Some Evidence on Structure 1878-1905." Ph.D. dissertation, University of California, (Riverside), 1978.

Doti, Lynn Pierson and Larry Schweikart. *Banking in the American West.* Norman, Oklahoma: University of Oklahoma Press, 1991.

Douglass, Elisha. *The Coming of Age of American Business.* Chapel Hill: University of North Carolina Press, 1971.

Dowd, Douglas. "A Comparative Analysis of Economic Development in the American West and South." *Journal of Economic History* 16 (December 1956): 558-574.

Duncan, Beverly and Stanley Lieberson. *Metropolis and Region in Transition.* Beverly Hills, California: Sage Publications, 1970.

Easterbrook, W.T. "Problems in the Relationship of Communication and Economic History." *Journal of Economic History* 20 (December 1960): 559-565.

Easterlin, Richard. "Regional Growth of Income." in Simon Kuznets and Dorothy Swaine Thomas, eds. *Population Redistribution and Economic Growth, United States, 1870-1950*, II. Philadelphia: American Philosophical Society, 1960.

Easterlin, Richard. "Regional Income Trends." in Robert Fogel and Stanley Engerman, eds. *The Reinterpretation of American Economic History*. New York: Harper & Row, 1971.

Easterlin, Richard. "State Income Estimates." in Simon Kuznets and Dorothy Swaine Thomas, eds. *Population Redistribution and Economic Growth, United States, 1870-1950*, I. Philadelphia: American Philosophical Society, 1957.

Eichengreen, Barry. "Mortgage Rates in the Populist Era." *American Economic Review* 74 (December 1984): 995-1015.

Elgie, Robert. "The Development of San Francisco Manufacturing, 1848-1880: An Analysis of Regional Locational Factors and Urban Spatial Structure." M.A. thesis, University of California, 1966.

Fishlow, Albert. "Antebellum Interregional Trade Reconsidered." *American Economic Review* 54 (May 1964): 352-364.

Fogel, Robert. "Railroads and American Economic Growth" in Robert Fogel and Stanley Engerman, eds. *The Reinterpretation of American Economic History*. New York: Harper & Row, 1971.

Fogel, Robert and Stanley Engerman, eds. *The Reinterpretation of American Economic History*. New York: Harper & Row, 1971.

Fogel, Robert and Jack Rutner. "The Efficiency Effects of Federal Land Policy, 1850-1900: A Report of Some Provisional Findings." in William Aydelotte, et al., eds. *The Dimensions of Quantitative Research in History*. Princeton: Princeton University Press, 1972.

Frederiksen, D. M. "Mortgage Banking in America." *Journal of Political Economy* 2 (December 1893): 203-234.

Friedman, Milton and Anna Jacobson Schwartz. *A Monetary History of the United States, 1867-1960*. Princeton: Princeton University Press, 1963.

Garnsey, Morris. *America's New Frontier: The Mountain West*. New York: Alfred Knopf, 1950.

Gerschenkron, Alexander. *Economic Backwardness in Historical Perspective*. New York: Frederick Praeger, 1965.

Gilbert, James. "Trade and Currency in Early Oregon." *Columbia University Studies in History, Economics, and Public Law* 26 (1907).

Goldsmith, Raymond. *Financial Structure and Development.* New Haven: Yale University Press, 1969.

Gras, N.S.B. *An Introduction to Economic History.* New York: Harper and Brothers, 1922.

Greef, Albert. *The Commercial Paper House in the United States.* New York: Arno Press, 1975.

Green, George. *Finance and Economic Development in the Old South.* Stanford: Stanford University Press, 1972.

Gurley, John and Edward Shaw. "Financial Aspects of Economic Development." *American Economic Review* 45 (September 1955): 515-538.

Gurley, John and Edward Shaw. "The Growth of Debt and Money in the United States, 1800-1950." *Review of Economics and Statistics* 39 (August 1957): 250-262.

Hartland, Penelope. "Interregional Payments Compared with International Payments." *Quarterly Journal of Economics* 63 (August 1949): 392-407.

Hedges, James. *Henry Villard and the Railways of the Northwest.* New Haven: Yale University Press, 1930.

Henderson, John. "Regional Differentials in Interest Rates." *Southern Economic Journal* 11 (October 1944): 113-132.

Hidy, Ralph, Frank Hill and Allan Nevins. *Timber and Men: The Weyerhaeuser Story.* New York: Macmillan, 1963.

Hochwald, Werner. "Conceptual Issues of Regional Income Estimation." in Conference on Research in Income and Wealth. *Regional Income.* Princeton: Princeton University Press, 1957.

Hunt, Reed. *Pulp, Paper and Pioneers: The Story of Crown Zellerbach Corporation.* New York: The Newcomen Society, 1961.

Hunter, James. *Partners in Progress 1864-1950: A Brief History of the Bank of California.* New York: The Newcomen Society, 1950.

Hurwitz, Abner and Carlyle P. Stallings. "Interregional Differentials in Per Capita Real Income Change." in Conference on Research in Income and Wealth. *Regional Income.* Princeton: Princeton University Press, 1957.

Isard, Walter. "Interregional and Regional Input-Output Analysis: A Model of a Space-Economy." *Review of Economics and Statistics* 33 (November 1951): 318-328.

Isard, Walter and Tze Hsiung Tung. "Some Concepts for the Analysis of Spatial Organization." *Papers and Proceedings of the Regional Science Association* 11 (1963): 17-40; 12 (1964): 1-25.

Jackson, W. Turrentine. *The Enterprising Scot.* Edinburgh: Edinburgh University Press, 1968.

Jackson, W. Turrentine. "Portland: Wells Fargo's Hub for the Pacific Northwest." *Oregon Historical Quarterly* (Fall 1985): 229-265.

Jackson, W. Turrentine. "Salt Lake City: Wells Fargo's Transportation Depot during the Stagecoach Era." *Utah Historical Quarterly* 53 (Winter 1985): 4-39.

Jackson, W. Turrentine. *Wells Fargo & Co. in Idaho Territory.* Boise: Idaho State Historical Society, 1984.

Jacobs, Jane. *Cities and the Wealth of Nations.* New York: Random House, 1984.

James, John. "Banking Market Structure, Risk, and the Pattern of Local Interest Rates in the United States, 1893-1911." *Review of Economics and Statistics* 58 (November 1976): 453-462.

James, John. "The Development of the National Money Market, 1893-1911." *Journal of Economic History* 36 (December 1976): 878-897.

James, John. "The Evolution of the National Money Market 1888-1911." Ph.D. dissertation, MIT, 1974.

James, John. "Financial Underdevelopment in the Postbellum South." *Journal of Interdisciplinary History* 11 (Winter 1981): 443-454.

James, John. *Money and Capital Markets in Postbellum America.* Princeton: Princeton University Press, 1978.

James, John and Jonathan Skinner. "Sources of Saving in the Nineteenth Century United States." Paper prepared for the Wesleyan Economic History Symposium, March 1985.

Johansen, Dorothy and Charles Gates. *Empire of the Columbia.* New York: Harper and Brothers, 1957.

Johnson, Arthur and Barry Supple. *Boston Capitalists and Western Railroads.* Cambridge: Harvard University Press, 1967.

Kearl, J.R. and Clayne Pope. "The Life Cycle in Economic History." *Journal of Economic History* 43 (March 1983): 149-158.

Keehn, Richard. "Federal Bank Policy, Bank Market Structure, and Bank Performance: Wisconsin, 1863-1914." *Business History Review* 48 (Spring 1974): 1-27.

Keehn, Richard and Gene Smiley. "Mortgage Lending by National Banks." *Business History Review* 51 (Winter 1977): 474-491.

Keleher, Robert. "Regional Credit Market Integration: A Survey and Empirical Examination." Working Paper Series, Federal Reserve Bank of Atlanta, February 1979.

Kemmerer, Edwin. *Seasonal Variations in the Relative Demand for Money and Capital in the United States.* Washington, D.C.: Government Printing Office, 1910.

Kindleberger, Charles. *Economic Response.* Cambridge: Harvard University Press, 1978.

Kindleberger, Charles. *Manias, Panics, and Crashes.* London: Macmillan Press, 1978.

King, Joseph. *History of the San Francisco Stock and Exchange Board.* San Francisco: J.L. King, 1910.

Kniffin, William. *The Practical Work of a Bank*, 9th edition. Cambridge: Bankers Publishing Company, 1948.

Knight, N.R. "Pioneer Private Bankers in Washington." *Washington Historical Quarterly* 25 (October 1934): 243-252.

Kuznets, Simon and Dorothy Swaine Thomas, eds. *Population Redistribution and Economic Growth, United States, 1870-1950.* 3 volumes. Philadelphia: American Philosophical Society, 1957, 1960, 1964.

Lamoreaux, Naomi. "Banks, Kinship, and Economic Development: The New England Case." *Journal of Economic History* 46 (September 1986): 647-667.

Lee, Susan Previant and Peter Passell. *A New Economic View of American History.* New York: Norton, 1979.

Lee, Virgil. *Principles of Agricultural Credit.* New York: McGraw-Hill, 1930.

Leff, Nathaniel. "Capital Markets in the Less Developed Countries: The Group Principle." in Ronald McKinnon, ed. *Money and Finance in Economic Growth and Development.* New York: Marcel Dekker, 1976.

Leven, Maurice. *Income in the Various States.* New York: National Bureau of Economic Research, 1925.

Lewis, Oscar. *The Big Four.* New York: Alfred Knopf, 1938.

Lewis, Oscar. *Silver Kings*. New York: Alfred Knopf, 1947.
Life Insurance Association of America. *Life Insurance Companies as Financial Institutions*. Englewood Cliffs, New Jersey: Prentice-Hall, 1962.
Lindstrom, Diane. *Economic Development in the Philadelphia Region, 1810-1850*. New York: Columbia University Press, 1978.
Lister, Roger. "Bank Behavior, Regulation, and Economic Development: California, 1860-1910." Ph.D. dissertation, University of California (Davis), 1982.
Lomax, Alfred. *Pioneer Woolen Mills in Oregon*. Portland, Oregon: Binfords and Mort, 1941.
Loomis, Noel. *Wells Fargo*. New York: Clarkson Potter, 1968.
Lösch, August. *The Economics of Location*. New Haven: Yale University Press, 1954.
Lotchin, Roger. *San Francisco, 1846-1856: From Hamlet to City*. New York: Oxford University Press, 1974.
Macaulay, Frederick. *Some Theoretical Problems Suggested by the Movements of Interest Rates*. New York: National Bureau of Economic Research, 1938.
Madison, James. "The Evolution of Commercial Credit Reporting Agencies in Nineteenth-Century America." *Business History Review* 48 (Summer 1974): 164-186.
Martin, Robert. *National Income in the United States, 1799-1938*. New York: National Industrial Conference Board, 1939.
McKinnon, Ronald. *Money and Capital in Economic Development*. Washington, D.C.: Brookings, 1973.
McWilliams, Carey. *California: The Great Exception*. New York: A.A. Wyn, 1949.
Michie, R.C. "The London Stock Exchange and the British Securities Market, 1850-1914." *Economic History Review* second series, 38 (February 1985): 61-82.
Minsky, Hyman, ed. *California Banking in a Growing Economy: 1946-1975*. Berkeley: Institute of Business and Economic Research, 1965.
Modigliani, Franco and Richard Sutch. "Debt Management and the Term Structure of Interest Rates: An Empirical Analysis of Recent Experience." *Journal of Political Economy* 85 (Supplement, August 1967): 569-589.

Modigliani, Franco and Richard Sutch. "Innovations in Interest Rate Policy." *American Economic Review* 56 (May 1966): 178-197.

Moore, C.I.D. *The Pacific Mutual Life Insurance Company of California*. Los Angeles: Pacific Mutual Life Insurance Company, 1928.

Myers, Margaret. *The New York Money Market*. New York: Columbia University Press, 1931.

Myrdal, Gunnar. *Economic Theory and Under-Developed Regions*. London: Duckworth, 1957.

Nadeau, Remi. *Los Angeles: From Mission to Modern City*. New York: Longmans, Green, and Co., 1960.

Nash, Gerald. *State Government and Economic Development*. Berkeley: Institute of Government Studies, 1964.

Neal, Larry. *The Rise of Financial Capitalism*. Cambridge: Cambridge University Press, 1990.

North, Douglass. "International Capital Flows and the Development of the American West." *Journal of Economic History* 16 (December 1956): 493-505.

North, Douglass. "Location Theory and Regional Economic Growth." *Journal of Political Economy* 63 (June 1955): 243-258.

Odell, Kerry. "The Integration of Regional and Interregional Capital Markets: Evidence from the Pacific Coast." *Journal of Economic History* 49 (June 1989): 297-310.

Odell, Kerry. "William Chapman Ralston and the Golden Beginnings of Finance on the Pacific Coast." Paper presented to Bancroft Readers' Roundtable, Berkeley, June 1986.

Odell, Kerry and David F. Weiman. "Regional Metropolitan Development and Financial Market Integration in the New South." Paper presented at the Social Science History Association Meetings, New Orleans, November 1991.

Olmstead, Alan. *New York City Mutual Savings Banks, 1819-1861*. Chapel Hill: University of North Carolina Press, 1976.

Olsen, Erling. *International Trade Theory and Regional Income Differences, United States 1880-1950*. London: North-Holland, 1971.

Oregon State Bank Examiner. *Annual Report*. Salem, Oregon (various years).

Patterson, E.M. "Certain Changes in New York's Position as a Financial Center." *Journal of Political Economy* 21 (June 1913): 523-539.

Perloff, Harvey, Edgar Dunn, Eric Lampard, and Richard Muth. *Regions, Resources, and Economic Growth.* Baltimore: Johns Hopkins Press, 1960.

Pollard, Lancaster. "The Pacific Northwest." in Merrill Jensen, ed. *Regionalism in America.* Madison: University of Wisconsin Press, 1952.

Pomeroy, Earl. *The Pacific Slope.* New York: Alfred Knopf, 1965.

Popple, Charles S. *Development of Two Bank Groups in the Central Northwest.* Cambridge: Harvard University Press, 1944.

Porter, Glenn and Harold Livesay. *Merchants and Manufacturers.* Baltimore: Johns Hopkins Press, 1971.

Pred, Allan. *The Spatial Dynamics of U.S. Urban-Industrial Growth, 1800-1914.* Cambridge: MIT Press, 1966.

Pritchett, Bruce. *A Study of Capital Mobilization: The Life Insurance Industry of the Nineteenth Century.* New York: Arno Press, 1977.

Quiett, Glenn. *They Built the West.* New York: Cooper Square, 1965.

Ralston, William Chapman. Personal correspondence, 1864-1875. Manuscript, Bancroft Library, University of California, Berkeley.

Rand McNally Co. *The Banker's Directory of the United States and Canada.* Chicago: Rand McNally and Company, annual.

Ransom, Roger and Richard Sutch. *One Kind of Freedom: The Economic Consequences of Emancipation.* Cambridge: Cambridge University Press, 1977.

Ransom, Roger and Richard Sutch. "Domestic Saving as an Active Constraint on Capital Formation in the American Economy, 1839-1928: A Provisional Theory." Working Papers on the History of Saving, #1. Berkeley: Institute of Business and Economic Research, December 1984.

Richardson, Harry W. *Regional Growth Theory.* New York: John Wiley and Sons, 1973.

Riefler, Winfield. *Money Rates and Money Markets in the United States.* New York: Harper and Brothers, 1930.

Robbins, Sidney and Nestor Terleckyj. *Money Metropolis.* Cambridge: Harvard University Press, 1960.

Robertson, Ross. *The Comptroller and Bank Supervision.* Washington, D.C.: The Office of the Comptroller of the Currency, 1968.

Rockoff, Hugh. "The Capital Market in the 1850s." Working Paper Series on Historical Factors in Long Run Growth, #11. Cambridge: National Bureau of Economic Research, January 1990.

Rockoff, Hugh. "Regional Interest Rates and Bank Failures, 1870-1914." *Explorations in Economic History* 14 (January 1977): 90-95.

Romans, J. Thomas. *Capital Exports and Growth Among U.S. Regions.* Middletown, Connecticut: Wesleyan University Press, 1965.

Rosenbloom, Joshua. "One Market or Many? Labor Market Integration in the Late Nineteenth-Century United States." *Journal of Economic History* 50 (March 1990): 85-107.

Rothstein, Morton. "A British Firm on the American West Coast, 1869-1914." *Business History Review* 37 (Winter 1963): 392-415.

Rothstein, Morton. "The California 'Wheat Kings'." Working Paper #22, Agricultural History Center, University of California (Davis), July 1985.

Rubin, Julius. "Canal or Railroad? Imitation and Innovation in the Response to the Erie Canal in Philadelphia, Baltimore, and Boston." *Transactions of the American Philosophical Society*, new series. 51 (7), November 1961.

Saunders, Margery. "California Wheat, 1867-1910: Influences of Transportation on the Export Trade and the the Location of Producing Areas." M.A. thesis, University of California, 1960.

Scheiber, Harry, Harold Vatter, and Harold Faulkner. *American Economic History.* New York: Harper & Row, 1976.

Schumpeter, Joseph. *The Theory of Economic Development.* Cambridge: Harvard University Press, 1934.

Sexton, Robert. "The Effect of Alternative Regional Delineations on Historical Interpretation." *Economic Forum* 12 (Winter 1981-1982): 77-83.

Simpson, Paul. *Regional Aspects of Business Cycles and Special Studies of the Pacific Northwest.* Study prepared for the Bonneville Administration, Eugene, Oregon, 1953.

Smiley, Wm. Gene. "The Evolution and Structure of the National Banking System, 1870-1913." Ph.D. dissertation, University of Iowa, 1973.

Smiley, Gene. "Interest Rate Movement in the United States, 1888-1913." *Journal of Economic History* 35 (September 1975): 591-620.

Smith, Woodruff. "The Function of Commercial Centers in the Modernization of European Capitalism." *Journal of Economic History* 44 (December 1984): 985-1005.

Snowden, Kenneth. "Mortgage Lending and American Urbanization, 1880-1890." *Journal of Economic History* 48 (June 1988): 273-285.

Snowden, Kenneth. "Mortgage Rates and American Capital Market Development in the Late Nineteenth Century." *Journal of Economic History* 47 (September 1987): 671-691.

Stigler, George. "Imperfections in the Capital Market." *Journal of Political Economy* 75 (June 1967): 287-292.

Sturm, James. *Investing in the United States, 1798-1893.* New York: Arno Press, 1977.

Sushka, Marie and Brian Barrett. "Banking Structure and the National Capital Market, 1869-1914." Atlanta: Georgia Institute of Technology, September, 1983. Photocopy.

Sushka, Marie and Brian Barrett. "Banking Structure and the National Capital Market, 1869-1914." *Journal of Economic History* 44 (June 1984): 463-477.

Sutch, Richard and Kerry Ann Odell. "Estimating Capital Stocks by State: Rhode Island, A Case Study, 1850-1910." History of Saving Research Memorandum #2, Berkeley: Institute of Business and Economic Research, September 1984.

Swanson, Joseph and Jeffrey Williamson. "Explanations and Issues: A Prospectus for Quantitative Economic History." *Journal of Economic History* 31 (March 1971): 43-57.

Sylla, Richard. "Federal Policy, Banking Market Structure, and Capital Mobilization in the United States, 1863-1913." *Journal of Economic History* 29 (December 1969): 657-686.

Tattersall, James. "The Economic Development of the Pacific Northwest to 1920." Ph.D. dissertation, University of Washington, 1960.

Throckmorton, Arthur. "The Role of the Merchant on the Oregon Frontier: The Early Business Career of Henry W. Corbett, 1851-1869." *Journal of Economic History* 16 (December 1956): 539-550.

U.S. Bureau of the Census. *Historical Statistics of the United States: Colonial Times to 1970.* Washington, D.C.: Government Printing Office, 1975.

U.S. Bureau of the Census. Tenth Census, volume 7: *Report on Valuation.* Washington, D.C.: Government Printing Office, 1884.

U.S. Bureau of the Census. Tenth Census, volume 19, part 2: *Social Statistics of Cities.* Washington, D.C.: Government Printing Office.

U.S. Bureau of the Census. Eleventh Census, volume 12, part II: *Report on Insurance Business in the United States.* Washington, D.C.: Government Printing Office, 1895.

U.S. Bureau of the Census. *Report on Real Estate Mortgages in the U.S. at the Eleventh Census.* Washington, D.C.: Government Printing Office, 1895.

U.S. Comptroller of the Currency. *Annual Report.* Washington, D.C.: Government Printing Office (various years).

U.S. Congress, Senate. *Banking and Currency Hearings on HR 7837: Bill to Provide for Establishment of Federal Reserve Banks.* 63rd Cong., 1st sess., 1913. S. Doc. 232, 3 vols.

U.S. Congress, Senate. Federal Bank Organization Committee. *Letter to the Federal Reserve Board Relative to the Location of the Federal Reserve Banks.* 63rd Cong., 2nd sess., 1914. S. Doc. 485.

Updike, Helen. "The National Banks and American Economic Development, 1870-1900." Ph.D. dissertation, State University of New York (Stony Brook), 1977.

Vance, James. *Geography and Urban Evolution in the San Francisco Bay Area.* Berkeley: Institute of Government Studies, 1964.

Vietorisz, Thomas. "Location Choices in Planning." in Max Millikan, ed. *National Economic Planning.* New York: National Bureau of Economic Research, 1967.

Walter, James. *The Role of Regional Security Exchanges.* Berkeley: University of California Press, 1957.

Washington State Banking Department. *Annual Report.* Olympia, Washington (various years).

White, Eugene. *The Regulation and Reform of the American Banking System, 1900-1929.* Princeton: Princeton University Press, 1983.

Williamson, Jeffrey. "Antebellum Urbanization in the American Northeast." *Journal of Economic History* 25 (December 1965): 592-608.

Williamson, Jeffrey. *Late Nineteenth-Century American Development: A General Equilibrium History.* London: Cambridge University Press, 1974.

Willis, Parker B. *The Federal Reserve Bank of San Francisco.* New York: Columbia University Press, 1937.

Wilson, Neil. *400 California Street.* San Francisco: The Bank of California, 1964.

Wright, Gavin. *Old South, New South.* New York: Basic Books, 1986.

Xander, James. *Vault Cash and the Role of Commercial Banks in Regional Economic Development.* New York: Arno Press, 1978.

Young, Allyn. "An Analysis of Bank Statistics for the United States." *Review of Economic Statistics* Part I: 6 (October 1924), 284-296; Part II: 7 (January 1925), 19-37; Part III: 7 (April 1925), 86-104.

INDEX